Intentional Living

A Personal Development Plan for the Experience Phase

Evan Raymer

Copyright © 2019 by Evan Raymer
All Rights Reserved

No part of this publication may be reproduced, distributed, or transmitted in any form or by any means, including photocopying, recording, or other electronic or mechanical methods, without the prior written permission of the publisher, except in the case of brief quotations embodied in critical reviews and certain other noncommercial uses permitted by copyright law.

Contents

Chapter 1: My Journey 1

Chapter 2: What is an Experience Phase? 3

Chapter 3: How to use this book 11

Chapter 4: Why Have Dedicated Phases? 13

Chapter 5: The Benefits of an Experience Phase 31

Chapter 6: Is it for Everyone? 41

Chapter 7: When to Start? 55

Chapter 8: Some Ideas for Experiences 65

Chapter 9: Planning and Choosing the Optimal Length 89

Chapter 10: Mindset and How to Act 95

Chapter 11: Guiding Someone Else 117

Chapter 12: What Next? 129

1
My Journey

My grandma loved to travel the world. When I was a toddler she would often come over to take care of me while my parents were working. I called her "Borneo Grandma" because she had lived in Malaysian Borneo for several months and worked with the famous orangutan scientist Birutė Galdikas.

We had a jigsaw puzzle which was designed in the shape of a world map. My grandma and I would spend hours putting it together over and over again. I often asked her questions about different parts of the world and she tried her best to answer. Even though she had been to a lot of countries she obviously couldn't answer my questions about some of the obscure lesser known places like French Guiana or the Ross Sea.

In response to my curiosity she invented a character named Sneezer Bedeezer, an intrepid world traveler who explored the world in his hot air balloon. Despite his courage, resourcefulness, and intelligence, Sneezer had one flaw, whenever he got scared he started sneezing. Sneezer had a few trusty sidekicks like Joe, Yeti the Iceman, and Cougher Bedaugher (who coughed every time he got scared).

I was obsessed with her stories and had all the plot lines memorized. She continued to tell me these stories as I got older, even after my parents, brother, and I moved to a different city. Sometimes we wouldn't see each other for months at a time but I was always able to remind her about the specific details of Sneezer's adventures. These stories left me with a wanderlust which lasts to this day. I can remember when I was 16 years old dreaming of traveling on my own to places like Thailand or Brazil, but at the time it felt like a goal I would never actually achieve.

Fast forward a couple of years and here I am. I have somehow through sheer will and determination managed to live out the life of my dreams. I am convinced that the key to accomplishing anything comes down to having dedicated focused phases in your life. This book is specifically about one kind of phase, the experience phase.

I can remember deciding that I wanted to have an experience phase almost six years ago. I was about to graduate from University and wasn't sure what I should focus on next. While some people actually have their experience phase in University, most of my dreams involved going away to new places and exploring the world. During my 5-year long experience phase I traveled to 33 countries, learned to speak new languages, and lived a lifestyle I never thought possible. In this book I will help you create a personal development plan to have an experience phase in your own life.

Recently, the last time I saw my grandma, she asked me to write a book. I had been mulling over the idea of writing a book for a long time, but her asking me was the last push that I needed. Without knowing what the book would be about I agreed to write one on the spot. After receiving a lot of positive feedback on an article I wrote about the experience phase in life I decided that it would be a perfect topic for a book.

This isn't just a motivational essay on pursuing your dreams, instead it is an entire approach to living life. The Experience Phase is just one of many different dedicated phases which are available to us. After reading this book you can decide whether or not it is the right time for you to have an Experience Phase, or if you are more interested in trying one of the other dedicated phases.

2
What Is an Experience Phase?

The Experience Phase is a preset period of time, anywhere from 2 months to 10 years, where you concentrate as much energy and focus as possible into having new experiences with the limitation that you should maintain to the best of your ability the other important aspects of your life.

This concept is already formalized in some cultures with the idea of a gap year. However, one year is probably a bit short for most people. Assuming that you live at least 70 years there is no reason why you can't dedicate a few more years to your experience phase. Although one year might not be enough for everyone, it will be fine for others. I will talk about choosing the right length of time for your experience phase in a later chapter. While not perfect for most people, the gap-year tradition is certainly in the right ballpark. Either way, if you are undertaking a gap-year or if you are scheduling an experience phase at a different point in your life, this book will provide you with the information that you need.

Ultimately, these experiences are about getting out of your comfort zone. That's generally what new experiences are all about. In a sense, that is the definition of a new experience. If it was inside your comfort zone, then it wouldn't be a new experience after all. So really the goal of an experience phase is to get out of your comfort zone, not just in one way, but in a multitude of different ways.

You also create your own opportunities, you can't just rely on the people around you. Sure it is important to accept the experiences that they offer, but it is also important to be independent and make things happen yourself. After all, other people might not share the same dreams as you.

In your experience phase not only do you get out of your comfort zone, but you also give yourself the opportunity to live out your dreams in reality. Throughout the course of their lives most people only get to live out a few of their dreams, some people don't live through any at all. During an experience phase you will live through as many of them as possible within the allotted time. You will get the chance to do all kinds of different things you never really thought you would actually do, things you only imagined in your mind.

The only dreams you won't be able to live out are those that are extremely dangerous to yourself, other people, or dreams which are literally physically impossible. Otherwise, I believe that if there is a will there's a way.

Many extraordinarily successful people have had life-changing experience phases. Some of them actually credit these experiences to being the foundation of their success, while others simply look back at their experience phases fondly. Before his success in business, Steve Jobs undertook an extensive spiritual journey which included intense meditative study and a seven month trip to India. He credited many of the experiences he had during this phase to helping him achieve success in business.

An experience phase isn't just about "getting it out of your system". This is a very bleak way of looking at it. In a sense that is true, one of the benefits of an experience phase is that it allows you to redirect your focus onto something else. For example, family, career, community, etc. But, in my opinion the experience phase is also valuable in its own right.

While you will probably gain a lot of wisdom and general insight from all of your experiences, that is only part of the reason why we do it. These experiences are simply intrinsically valuable. You don't have to get anything out of them, you don't have to tell anyone else, you simply have the experience and the memories and that's what is important. Later on in this book I will go into more detail into the pragmatic benefits of different experiences. But I wonder, what is the point of being alive if not for the experiences we have while we are here?

That's not to say that you shouldn't try to gain some kind of wisdom from your experiences, in fact the wisdom you gain will be invaluable for the rest of your life. By my temperament, I am a very pragmatic person, and you might be the same way as well. For people like us it is important to remember to appreciate experiences for what they are, interestingly this is the best way to get some kind of value out of the experiences.

When you appreciate experiences for what they are intrinsically you are able to pay more attention and understand those experiences in a more fundamental way. If, during an experience, you are constantly thinking about the potential pragmatic applications of that experience, you diversify your focus and as a result are unable to fully immerse yourself in the activity.

Half-way through my experience phase I became obsessed with learning blindfold chess. This is where you play the entire chess game in your head without looking at the board at all. Every chess move has a code i.e. knight to e5 or bishop to f7. This way you can communicate your chess moves to the other player whether or not they are using an actual board.

Blindfold chess requires a lot of concentration. I believe that I improved my own general ability to focus by learning to play chess in my head. But, while I was playing those blindfold chess games I wasn't thinking about the potential benefits, instead I was fully immersed in the games themselves. This allowed me to concentrate more deeply and actually gain more from the experience.

***

My own experiences have informed me in terms of my decision making more than anything else. I do try to learn from other people, but I think that we all value our own personal experiences more. That is just human nature.

One way that my experiences have informed my decisions is that I am now much more open to the idea of living the rest of my life in a foreign country. I used to be fairly certain that I would live in Canada long-term, but now this is no longer clear to me. While Canada is an amazing country with beautiful nature and a lot of economic opportunities, I can also see the potential in dozens of other places all over the world. Because of my travel experiences it is clear to me that there are a lot of wonderful places which are much more affordable than Canada and life there could make more logical sense.

Even if you don't see experiences as valuable in themselves, I am sure you can agree that experiences are important for other reasons. We all value and respect people with a lot of experiences, this is part of the reason why we respect elderly people so much. We understand that experiences make us wiser.

As I mentioned earlier when you experience something new you get out of your comfort zone. The important thing to note about the comfort zone is that it is constantly changing. When you do something that takes you out of your comfort zone, your comfort zone expands a bit because you become a bit more comfortable doing that new thing. When you do it over and over again it eventually becomes totally integrated into your new comfort zone. On the other hand, when you stay within your comfort zone it gradually contracts over time, this is what is meant by people being "set in their ways".

People who keep doing the same things day after day will only be comfortable doing those things that they do every single day. The things which used to be on the border of their comfort zone gradually become more and more uncomfortable.

Imagine someone who is slightly uncomfortable introducing themselves to new people, but they make it a habit to meet new people occasionally. Now picture that this same person stops getting out of their comfort zone and stops meeting new people entirely, chances are that they will soon become very uncomfortable introducing themselves to new people or doing other things which they used to be kind of comfortable doing.

On the other hand, if instead of avoiding new people they make a habit of introducing themselves to new people every single day, pretty soon they will become totally comfortable doing it. Your comfort zone grows and contracts depending on what you spend your time doing.

***

An experience which immediately took me out of my comfort zone was traveling to developing countries alone, I started off in Tulum, Mexico. Tulum is actually very touristic and is quite developed compared to a lot of the other countries that I have visited since, but for me at the time just traveling abroad solo was a transformative experience. In the beginning of this trip I had negotiated 3 months off work with my employer to backpack through Central America, I stayed in contact with my manager throughout the trip and we agreed that I could continue traveling for an additional three months.

In total I traveled for 6 months through 8 countries and I made it all the way to Bolivia. My life has never been the same since. Nowadays, traveling doesn't take me out of my comfort zone like it used to. I have been all around Europe, Asia, Africa, and South America and actually feel at home almost anywhere. While I have completed my own personal experience phase, I still want to make sure that I am always doing things which take me out of my comfort zone.

Another experience which took me out of my comfort zone was going to Burning Man in 2016. I have always been a natural introvert, while I am not particularly shy I do certainly like to spend a lot of time alone. Perhaps this is why I enjoy writing so much. If you don't already know about Burning Man here is a quick run-down. It is a huge week-long festival in the desert in Nevada with more than 70 000 people.

In my estimation, Burning Man is an experimental Utopia exploring how people can live and interact with each other. There are ten core principles at the festival, I am not going to bore you by explaining all ten principles, but one of these main principles is "participation". Normally, when I go to big events, I prefer to sit back and watch. This isn't really an option and certainly isn't in the spirit of Burning Man. I ended up having to participate and actually ended up enjoying participating.

One of my favorite places at Burning Man is a Boeing 747 airliner which has been converted into an art exhibit. To enter the airplane you need to pass through the "insecurity checkpoint" where you write down your insecurities on the "emotional baggage" tags before entering.

This art project hits the nail on the head. When you know your insecurities you know where you need to go next. Your insecurities are like a dowsing rod, they point outside of your comfort zone.

I am still deciding on my next big project to get out of my comfort zone. It may be learning paragliding, but that will depend on the way the rest of my life goes. Either way, we all have insecurities and we all have a comfort zone, but overcoming our comfort zone is one of the most incredible experiences available to us.

I believe that experience phases can vary quite a bit from person to person. For some people their experience phase might only last a few months and for others it could last a whole decade. Also, they vary quite a bit in terms of what people do. For me, it was all about travel and meditation, others might appreciate something similar or something very different. A lot of people become surf / ski / dive / climbing / hiking / martial arts enthusiasts. They find some temporary work near the perfect spot to practice their craft, stay in very cheap (usually shared) accommodation, eat basic food, and have the time of their lives.

Another excellent path is more spiritually focused. While it is common to head out on an adventure exploring the outside world, many people find that the inner world is even more expansive. Those who dedicate themselves to studying their own consciousness inevitably discover the enormous range of experiences available within the human mind. There are many stories from many different religions where people undertook a spiritually focused experience phase, in fact, in some cases this experience phase was the origin of the religion itself. Consider taking on a spiritual experience phase and visiting those holy sites, spiritual schools, and/or the recesses of your own mind that you always wanted to explore.

***

For many people their own path is very clear, in fact, this is the way it was for me. I have always had a strong sense of what I need to do, the tricky part is usually the details. For other people knowing the general arc of their experience phase can be a bit more challenging. This is why I have a chapter on what to do during your experience phase with a number of different ideas and how to choose which of these paths is ideal for you.

Almost everyone who goes through an experience phase will dramatically expand their comfort zone in one direction. In order to go through an experience phase you will probably have to cut costs quite a bit, perhaps with extreme measures depending on your particular financial situation. The good news is that living on the bare minimum is actually an interesting experience in itself and isn't even that unpleasant once you get used to it.

One benefit I experienced from budget travel is that I realized that I can be happy with almost no money. There are people who travel on less than a few dollars a day and they don't seem any less happy than anyone else. Of course, going from spending 100 000 dollars a year to spending 10 000 dollars a year will mean a lot of discomfort, but the human mind is incredibly adaptable and you will be surprised how quickly you get used to the new standard of living.

My main goal with this book is helping people make their dreams a reality. I can remember when my own dreams seemed abstract and farfetched. Not only to me, but also to the people around me. It is very realistic for you to live out your dreams as well. Something special happens in your mind when you commit to taking on an experience phase, it's like all the challenges and difficulties move aside. The commitment you must make and the limited time frame are very critical, I will discuss this more later on.

3
How to use this Book

When I read a book I don't always read it in chronological order, sometimes I scan through certain sections and I reread other sections more carefully. You should do the same with this book, read it however you see fit. If you have the physical copy write notes in it, fold the pages. If something I say sounds wrong be critical, if something I say sounds right be even more critical. Not everything I say is correct, in fact despite the care I put into this book I probably made a lot of mistakes so don't take anything I say at face value. Feel free to close the book at any time to go for a walk and consider what I said or call up a friend you respect and ask them what they think.

Skip a section if it doesn't apply to you, but remember to go back and read it later on in your life when it does apply. You can always read the book from start finish if you'd like, after all there is a logical order to the way I structured things, or you can just choose the chapters which appeal to you and focus on them. As I explain later on I am a strong believer that everyone is different and everyone should live their life differently, this applies to reading as well as life. Use the book in whatever way feels right to you.

4
Why Have Dedicated Phases?

Concentrating on a single aspect of your life for a period of time might appear a strange way to live, but it is actually an excellent option for a lot of people. It seems like most people in the greater society actually live in a more balanced way, concentrating on nearly every single aspect of their life at the same time. But, as I will explain later, dedicated phases don't necessarily mean that you have to live an unbalanced life.

The most fundamental reason why you have an intentional phase is because it allows you to pursue that part of your life in a much deeper way. Normally, I only read casually when I have the time, but during my 5-year intellectual phase I would go deep into obscure philosophical texts and academic research papers, for no reason other than pure curiosity. During my experience phase I was able to push my boundaries and pursue diverse goals like meditating for hours on end or moving to new countries to learn their languages. People living more ordinary lives can't simply move to a new country to pursue some whimsical goal like learning a new language. However, during an experience phase you have this freedom.

I should make a caveat before going any further. Extreme life focus on one topic or pursuit has always come naturally to me. My mom tells me that when I was a toddler I had hundreds of different birds memorized from a bird watcher's encyclopedia that we owned. Later on I became obsessed with chess and played in tournaments regularly. Despite this potential personal bias, I still believe that dedicated phases are a good idea for a lot of people, especially at certain points in their lives.

***

Here are some examples to help you understand what I mean by a dedicated phase. There are endless options for different kinds of life phases, I am certainly not claiming that this is an exhaustive list. Feel free to get creative and come up with your own phases or make modifications on the phases I listed.

Career Phase: A period of time where someone dedicates as much energy as possible into progressing in their career. This could mean working very long hours or taking courses on top of a regular job. A career phase would make sense for someone with limited obligations who also knows exactly what they want to do for a career. A great time to organize a career phase is at the point where the stakes are highest, meaning that your performance will dictate the future course of your career or how much money you will eventually earn.

The Intellectual/Philosophical Phase: When someone concentrates all their effort into learning, exploring new ideas, and understanding the nature of reality. For some people this is what University is all about, others undertake an intellectual phase at various points in their life. While I don't believe that it is possible to make much progress in terms of answering the main philosophical questions in a satisfying way, the intellectual phase does benefit people in terms of improving their overall cognitive abilities.

The Spiritual Phase: Spirituality and religion seem to be fundamental to the human experience. While some people are much more "spiritual" than others, you won't encounter a lot of cultures without any kind of religion. Spirituality is seemingly a core human requirement similar to basic necessities like food, water, shelter etc. Spiritually inclined people could benefit from dedicating a few years to their spiritual practice.

Starting a Business: Think about the people you know who have started a very successful business, even if they don't work hard right now, they likely worked extremely hard in the beginning.

The Experience Phase: The title and point behind this book, don't worry we will get to this later.

Concentrating on a Specific Skill: Focusing on one specific skill/craft for a period of time. This could merge with an experience phase in certain circumstances. For example, moving to Bali for a few years to practice surfing might also be an experience phase for some people. On the other hand, practicing a specific skill might not involve new experiences at all. If someone were to focus on woodworking, they wouldn't even necessarily need to leave their house.

A Single Experience: I guess this is a type of experience phase, but instead of aiming for a wide breadth of experiences, you would have one very deep experience. An example would be living in the wilderness for a year.

***

Imagine someone is at a point in their lives where they are confident in their career choice, they have spent a few years in their profession already, and they are at a critical period for their long-term success. An example would be a tenure-track professor, if they are able to get over this career bump they will be set for the rest of their life.

This person might want to consider taking on a career phase until they get their tenure. Instead of pursuing that position casually and working 40-hours per week, they could put in 70-80 hours per week in an attempt to insure their long-term success. This might seem extreme to some people, but imagine how disappointed they would be if they didn't get the position because they had tried to live a so-called balanced life.

Another example would be someone who has either just finished University or has just moved out of their parents' house. They don't know what they want to do for a career so they are working a dead-end job which pays around minimum wage or slightly more.

For fun, let's say she has been training taekwondo (a Korean martial art) since she was 8 years old, loves Korean culture, and even has a Korean language app on her phone. Her work schedule is fairly unpredictable, sometimes she has to work in the evenings, sometimes on the weekends and as a result she ends up missing a lot of taekwondo practices.

Even though she is a black belt, she is frustrated that she doesn't get to practice as much as she used to. While she watches Korean entertainment on her computer she only has a few Korean friends who she sees every couple of weeks. Sometimes she gets into the habit of practicing Korean every day on her phone, but usually these streaks only last a few weeks and then she goes months without practicing at all. Despite trying to learn Korean for the last couple of years, she has barely made any progress. Does this story sound familiar at all? You may be in a similar situation where you have been unable to pursue your passion because of other distractions in your life.

In my opinion, she would be wise to find work in Korea. Many people are able to find work teaching English there, other people find volunteer options. Perhaps her martial arts school could help her out. She might have to take a pay cut, but if she is willing to live in basic conditions I am confident she will be able to make it work.

When you commit to a dedicated phase discomforts become irrelevant, they brush past like a gust of wind. If you can handle discomfort you can overcome almost anything. Imagine how much money you could save if you doubled the amount of hours you work or took on a second job and saved every single extra penny that wasn't absolutely necessary for survival. This might seem unreasonable and crazy, and I will admit that it is probably unnecessarily extreme. But, the point I am making is that if you can handle discomfort you have unbelievable power. Taking on a dedicated phase makes discomfort much easier to overcome.

Every worthwhile pursuit has associated discomforts, in fact, everything that is great in life is sometimes uncomfortable. Usually the greater that thing is, the more uncomfortable it is. Why is this the case?

I believe that it all comes down to the concept of homeostasis in biology. This is one of the deepest and most fundamental principles in biological systems. The Khan Academy defines homeostasis as "…the tendency to resist change in order to maintain a stable, relatively constant internal environment." So basically, if you try to change, your body/brain says "No!". But here is the good part about homeostasis, if you keep doing the same new thing over and over again eventually your brain-body system will adapt and that will become the new normal for you. This is what is meant by expanding your comfort zone.

As I said earlier committing to a dedicated phase makes overcoming discomfort much easier. You simply won't experience nearly as much resistance. There are numerous reasons why.

You Are Able to Structure Your Life around the Goal:

Some people simply allow different patterns to emerge in their life, but I believe that it is generally better to control these patterns yourself. When you control and plan the patterns in your life you can optimize them to your specific goals.

When I was in my experience phase I met tons of new people, often we would stay up late talking and enjoying each other's company. It didn't make much sense to get up early, in fact, I found that my lifestyle was optimized when I was waking up between 10 a.m. - 11 a.m. But, when I want to write more effectively I find that I perform better when I wake up much earlier, sometimes before sunrise. When I commit to a phase, I can optimize my sleep schedule around that phase.

When you are in a new period in your life it is a good idea to find friends who share your new goals. Perhaps you are lucky and your old friends are trying to do the same things as you, but more likely you will need to find a few new people who are working in the same direction as you are. There is a common saying in many languages, which tends to go something like this "show me your friends, and I will show you who you are". I certainly recommend trying to maintain your closest friendships no matter which phase you are in, but that shouldn't stop you from meeting new people whose goals are coherent with your new phase.

Finding these friends is valuable for multiple reasons. They will share important information with you, including potential pitfalls and opportunities. Also, you are likely to get motivated by them and find that they can help you pursue your goals with more intensity. When you are having challenges with your goals your friends should provide support and motivation for overcoming those challenges.

For many people, travel is a phase in itself. But, travel can also assist in other phases. If you are committed to taking on a dedicated phase you have the option of traveling to the ideal place for that particular phase. For example, during a career phase you could travel to a new city for new job prospects. Or during a spiritual phase you could travel to a spiritual destination and live there for a while. This ability to travel for a specific goal is not typical for people living a more moderate lifestyle.

You take on the Appropriate Mentality for the Goal:

For each phase in life there are different mentalities which are key. During your experience phase you must constantly be thinking about how your current actions are working towards taking you out of your comfort zone. During an intellectual phase it is important to keep thinking about how you can improve your thought processes and find ways to learn faster and also understand concepts at a deeper level. During a financial phase you should always be thinking about how you can either earn more money or save more money. By taking on these mentalities as a moment to moment discipline you will find that you not only blast through the challenges, but you exceed your wildest expectations.

You Become Aggressive:

By aggressive I don't mean in a physical or animalistic way, but rather I am referring to pursuing your goals actively rather than hoping to achieve them by chance. When you are chasing a goal you will inevitably experience discomforts, but since you are intentionally taking on these discomforts they are much easier to deal with. Discomforts that you choose on purpose are much easier to deal with than discomforts you are forced to deal with by chance. Here is an example.

Imagine I told you that you had to sit perfectly still in a dark room for an hour and think about nothing, this would be a very unpleasant experience for a lot of people. However some people (myself included) find that long meditation sessions can be very enjoyable. Why is this? Sure the previous experience that we have doing meditation helps a lot, but also another reason why it is enjoyable for us is that we literally choose to do it.

Another example is exercise. Sometimes exercises, like pushups, are used as a punishment in certain situations such as the military. However, many people find all kinds of different exercise to be enjoyable. Even things which would seem boring to outsiders like weightlifting, running, cycling, or swimming laps. If most people were forced to do any of these things, it would be a punishment. Maybe at first the long-distance runner found her hobby painful, but now it brings her comfort. By actively choosing to run regularly she eventually learned to love doing it.

The same thing happens when you enter into a new phase. At first it hurts because it is uncomfortable, you are challenging your homeostasis. But, over time, your mind/body adapts and you no longer experience the discomfort (or maybe you even enjoy it).

Your Life has Purpose

Many people feel that they are living their lives aimlessly without any purpose. Have you heard Nietzsche's famous statement "God is dead"? This wasn't his aggressive way of saying that he is an atheist, rather he was expressing how the intellectual developments of the enlightenment killed the average person's belief in god.

In the present day many people are living without traditional sources of meaning such as religion, but also lifelong careers defined by previous family history, belief in objective morality, rigid caste structures, or even pure physical survival. While in some ways dropping these previously held sources of meaning has improved our societies, it has also left many people in a confused state of mind. Modern life is like a video game where you can't lose, but there is also no clear objective.

Two hundred years ago society might have given you your life path, but now we don't have that luxury. You need to give your own life meaning, and one way to do that is by turning your life into a story. Does your life have a coherent plot structure? Does the main character make heroic decisions? Or is your life story some kind of incoherent comedic tragedy like Samuel Beckett's Waiting for Godot?

When you organize your life into distinct dedicated phases it starts to take on more of a story structure. Instead of letting outside events dictate the course of your life, you can choose the plot structure by planning out dedicated phases. This is the ideal form of living intentionally, you take control of your own life.

The Advantages of Focus

Focus is unbelievably powerful. When has someone ever accomplished something great without focus? Listen to any great entrepreneur, they all say that in order to get a business off the ground it is necessary to work tirelessly spending every last moment of free time developing the business. Gary Vaynerchuck is famous for saying that first-time entrepreneurs should spend a minimum of 5 years literally doing nothing but work before even considering taking a break. Elon Musk recently said that when you first start a business you need to spend every waking moment working on it.

This focus applies to spiritual phases as well. Think about meditation retreats. Spiritual leaders in many religions are known to spend months in complete isolation simply focusing on their meditative practice. People who have undergone month long meditation retreats usually insist that they were able to reach states of consciousness unavailable to them during normal practice. In Christianity monks forego many worldly pleasures in order to dedicate themselves to their prayer. You will find a similar phenomenon in almost every single religion.

Scientific and philosophical pursuits also benefit from intense focus. Nikola Tesla stated that, "The mind is sharper and keener in seclusion and uninterrupted solitude. No big laboratory is needed in which to think. Originality thrives in seclusion free of outside influences beating upon us to cripple the creative mind. Be alone, that is the secret of invention; be alone, that is when ideas are born." and of course in his time there was no social media, Netflix, or YouTube, solitude was true focus. This is why some of the keenest minds and most powerful thinkers in human history were imbalanced and strange. In order to have the mental power necessary to produce ideas capable of transforming a scientific discipline, one must forego developing other aspects of one's life.

When you are living a moderate balanced life without a clear focus it is easy to get distracted by trivial things. Some people will get obsessed with TV shows, other people spend their time learning about comic book characters, another common distraction is social drama. While it is certainly possible to get distracted during any phase in your life, it is much easier to get distracted when you are living a balanced life. If you don't have a clear focus trivial matters can more easily pass undetected through your filters and enter into your mind, but when you allow yourself to take advantage of your tunnel vision these distractions usually won't have a chance to emerge.

Elite level competitive fighters often have training camps before their fights. They might even move to a new city to get away from their friends, family, and other responsibilities. This way they can concentrate all of their energy into the fight. If it wasn't effective, elite fighters wouldn't do it.

When we diversify our focus, it becomes much less powerful. You might say that it is better to keep your eggs in different baskets, but if you don't focus on one thing you risk losing at everything.

Falling into a Trap

Dedicated phases keep you from falling into a trap. Many people live their entire lives in one phase, this can cause a lot of problems. When you decide that you are going to spend a predefined amount of time in a particular phase it keeps you from getting stuck in that phase for your entire life.

What can happen is that you take on some pursuit and over time that pursuit becomes your identity. This is actually something you will intentionally take advantage of during a dedicated phase. But, if you are living unintentionally and just doing whatever pops up in front of you, it is very possible to get seduced by the new identity.

Bodybuilding is a perfect example, bear with me if you have no interest in bodybuilding. The sad story of many bodybuilders begins with them going to the gym to put on a bit of extra muscle. In the beginning they get pretty good results, people compliment them on their new physique, they get more romantic opportunities, and of course they are proud of their new awesome looking body. So they start taking the gym more seriously, eating better, training harder, and they get even more compliments and more benefits. Pretty soon bodybuilding becomes a part of their identity. But, with every skill, if you want to take it to the next level you have to make sacrifices.

Eventually it becomes very difficult to build more muscle naturally, so bodybuilders may turn to performance enhancing drugs. And again after taking these drugs everyone is complimenting them, they are getting attention on social media, and now they are the most muscular guy in their gym. At this point being a big muscular guy has become a fundamental part of their personality, they end up taking more drugs to get more results and the process repeats and repeats. Eventually they transform into some kind of monster and do irreversible damage to their body. You might think, "I have no interest of getting into bodybuilding". But, the same vicious cycle can happen with anything.

The pitfalls of spending your entire life in a financial phase have been widely explored in art including the film Citizen Kane and the book *a Christmas Carol*. The evil rich man is so widely used in different stories that the character has become a trope, this trope is actually exaggerated with comedic effect in the Simpsons (Mr. Burns). Jealous people love to stress how money doesn't make you happy, and they are right. While this trope is probably overdone, it is a very real risk for people who excessively pursue money their entire lives.

As someone who has taken on an intellectual phase for just over 5 years I believe I have some insight into the potential downsides of this kind of lifestyle. The problem is simple, you are just spinning your wheels. No matter how much time and energy you put into understanding the nature of reality you won't get anywhere. It's not even possible to make the slightest amount of progress. Does that mean that an intellectual phase is worthless? Not at all, the philosophy and science I learned during this period armed me with substantially improved cognitive skills. Also, there is no reason why you need to engage in an intellectual phase as broad as mine. Yours could be geared around a particular scientific question, in which case I believe that you are much more likely to get a sense of progress.

The Dangers of a Lifelong Experience Phase

To my knowledge, the potential dangers of spending your entire life in an experience phase have not been widely explored in art or literature. Mark Manson, the author of the *Subtle Art of not Giving a F*ck*, is the only person I know of who has written seriously about the dangers of a lifelong experience phase. In fact, the experience-based lifestyle is usually romanticized by artists.

Why has the experience phase not been vilified at all by artists? Probably because most artists score high on the Big Five Personality measure of openness to new experience. The Big Five Personality Inventory is one of the most well established concepts in psychology, the different traits can be consistently correlated to different aspects of people's lives. The following characteristics make up openness to new experience:

- Creativity
- Interest in Art
- Intellectual Curiosity
- Desire for Novelty
- Imagination
- Aesthetic Sensitivity

Since most artists score high on openness to new experience it's hard for them to understand why a life dedicated to pure experience could be bad. Due to my social group, my job, and my travels I have met a number of people in their 60s and 70s who dedicated their lives to having a wide breadth of experiences. Maybe this was because of their temperament, maybe it was because of their own social group, or maybe it was intentional, either way these people tend to have many of the same challenges.

Before going any further I want to be clear that most people who dedicate their lives to having a wide breadth of experiences also have a lot of positive qualities. They tend to be fun to be around, they make friends easily, have lots of awesome stories, and they have fascinating perspectives on the way the world works.

Now for the first downside. They rarely contribute to society. If you want to provide some kind of valuable contribution to your community, nation, or the world at large you need to commit to one thing for a fairly long period time. Or else you just won't develop the skills necessary to actually be useful. I am certainly not saying that you can't make a habit of getting out of your comfort zone for your entire life, the issue is with not dedicating enough time to one skill/profession to give back to the greater collective.

The other downside is a bit more sinister. In most modern societies the greatest dangers we have to face are addictions, things like alcohol, drugs, sex, social media, food, etc. The best shield we have against addictions is self-control. The problem with people who dedicate their entire lives to having a wide breadth of experiences is that they usually don't put in the decades required to develop a strong muscle of self-control. Also, these sorts of people tend to be risk-takers who don't mind trying out dangerous things. I think you can see where I am going with this...

A lot of the people I met who dedicated their entire lives to experiences are addicted to alcohol, drugs or other things. It's easy to romanticize flower-children but we tend to forget about what happened to Jimi Hendrix, Janis Joplin, or Jack Kerouac. These people actually contributed to the rest of society with their art, but many of those who live this lifestyle fade away into obscurity.

So back to dedicated phases, here is the point. When you set a predetermined amount of time for a particular phase you are less likely to fall into the trap of spending your entire life in that phase. When the period of time is over, you might struggle adapting to your new identity, but it is important to set limits so you don't stay in that phase for your entire life.

Note: some people intentionally and rationally choose to stay in one phase for their entire lives, in spite of the fact that it makes them unhappy. This is very common with scientists, mathematicians, philosophers and other thinkers. They feel that it is worth their while to concentrate on one thing for their entire lives for the purpose of discovering something that might improve the state of humanity, even if it means that they live an unbalanced and potentially unfulfilling life. Elon Musk is probably doing more to improve humanity than any other person on the planet, but he openly admits that his life is unpleasant. The level of focus and work required to produce as much as Musk would overwhelm most people very quickly, but he has maintained the intensity for decades.

I applaud these types of people who sacrifice their own happiness for the rest of humanity, but realistically most of us don't want to live our lives that way. And of course, if we actually lived like Musk, we simply wouldn't have the talent to make a fraction of the positive impact that he does. While I believe that it is important to contribute to the greater society at some point in our lives, there is no reason to sacrifice our happiness in the process.

The Problem with Work-life Balance

Work-life balance built around 40-hour work weeks has become a staple of modern society. This idea makes a lot of sense for people who are supporting a family, they don't want to be out of the house working all the time. But, for a single person with goals I see the concept of work-life balance as the worst of both worlds.

What I have noticed about most people who work a standard work week, anywhere from 35-50 hours per week, is that they don't have a lot of energy during their free time. I believe that some people are naturally very energetic and they can actually do something interesting after work, however this is the minority. Personally, if I were working a standard work week I would probably just want to watch Netflix when I get home and it would be a challenge to force myself to go out and do something.

This is why I prefer extreme working alternated with extreme living. My experience may be different from yours, but I find that the more I work the more I actually enjoy it! When I focus on working for a set period of time, I don't get burned out, rather I seem to gain momentum. Of course, this extreme working mentality gives me the freedom to pursue whatever kind of lifestyle I want.

Having dedicated phases doesn't mean that your life is necessarily imbalanced as a whole, it just means that it is imbalanced for a preset period of time. It would be perfectly reasonable to do one phase and then to schedule a completely different phase. Or you could go back to living more moderately. If anything, dedicated phases keep your life from becoming imbalanced because they prevent you from falling into a trap, i.e. focusing on one thing for your entire life instead of just a preset period of time.

The awesome thing about dedicated phases is that they give you the best of both worlds. They allow you to reach the intensity of an imbalanced person who focuses their entire lives around one goal, but at the same time they give you the moderation of a more balanced lifestyle.

Parkinson's Law

Intentionally planning out a dedicated phase helps you understand that phase in the context of the rest of your life. If you know that your next 5 years are dedicated to having a lot of interesting experiences and the next phase afterwards will be something entirely different, it gives you a kind of urgency. The urgency isn't necessarily stressful, but it is a boot in the right direction.

Parkinson's Law states that "work expands so as to fill the time available for its completion". Knowing that you have a limited amount of time to accomplish some goal is an incredibly powerful motivator. Have you ever noticed how procrastinators seem to be able to get an absurd amount of work done in the last few hours? Take advantage of this effect by setting yourself a time limit.

Manage Risks

Also, when you understand the phase within the context of the rest of your life it allows you to intelligently manage risks. When you have some ambiguous goal like "get out of my comfort zone more often", you don't really know how much getting out of your comfort zone is actually worth from a financial or safety perspective. Simply because it is hard to estimate the costs throughout the course of your entire life, but if you have a time limit you can do things like set yourself a monthly budget for new experiences. Or if you are starting a business you can give yourself a time limit to get it off the ground.

If you have the mentality that you will be in this phase forever you might take certain risks or burn bridges unnecessarily. For example, if you are focusing on your career your friends and family will be an annoying distraction. So if you imagine that you will be focusing on your career for the rest of your life you might decide to cut them off completely. When you recognize that this is just a phase, you will know that it is important to maintain your relationships while you build your career at the same time. I am not saying that you need to spend tons of time with them, in fact you can even see them much less frequently than you would otherwise. Maintaining is substantially easier than improving. The point is that you want to do enough to keep the relationships that you truly care about while focusing on some other goal.

Some people jump from phase to phase in their lives without knowing what they are doing. They might imagine that whatever phase they are in will last for life. The problem is that they burn bridges, destroy relationships, and lose many opportunities in the process. When they do inevitably move on to another stage they have to start over at square one.

A Sense of Meaning

Life stages are a fundamental part of being alive, in fact, many cultures have predefined life stages. The following is a life path you know very well, I'm not breaking ground here at all. Children start off living with their parents, then they go to elementary school, then high school, then possibly college, normally they go through an apprenticeship before undertaking a career, then they get married, buy a house, have kids, and eventually retire and die. This is the closest thing modern western culture has to a predefined series of dedicated phases. The reality is that this life path has become a joke, people don't take it seriously anymore and as a result it has lost its power. While many people were happy following this path in the past, in the modern day it's not profound enough, unfortunately most people won't get meaning following this life path anymore.

In many countries, particularly in the west, people don't have externally defined life phases. Sure there is college, but not everyone goes to college, and what you are supposed to be doing in college is getting increasingly ambiguous. It's unclear whether college is about career preparation, reading classic literature, learning esoteric intellectual ideas, or simply self-discovery.

Historically, and sometimes in the modern era, cultures understood the importance of dedicated life phases. Rather than leaving it up to individuals to create their own life phases, they defined these phases very clearly.

The Amish and Mennonite are a group of very traditional Christian fellowships who intentionally forego most modern technology. You might recognize them by their unique clothing or see them getting around by horse and buggy. Amish and Mennonite people live in close-knit communities and usually don't interact much with people from other religions. As you might expect they shun drugs, alcohol, and premarital sex.

Many Amish and Mennonite communities implement an experience phase called "Rumspringa". During this period adolescents are allowed to interact with outside communities, use drugs and alcohol, stay up late, party, have sex, and really do whatever they want. The period usually lasts 2 years depending on the community. Amazingly, after Rumspringa, the vast majority of Amish and Mennonite teenagers choose to get baptized and return to their more traditional lifestyle.

Historically, in most cultures, people were generally expected to get married and have children at a certain age. This is becoming less and less common all over the world, in fact many people are choosing to not have children at all. This is a perfect example of a culturally defined life phase which is quickly disappearing. Nowadays, it is up to individuals to decide if they want to have children or not. Overall, this personal autonomy is a good thing, but it also leaves people in a more confused state. As individuals become more and more autonomous in choosing the course of their own life, it is becoming increasingly critical for people to be intentional about their own life paths.

Periodization in Sports Training

When it comes to training athletes one of the most common principles is periodization. This is where an athlete's training regimen is organized into different phases e.g. a strength phase, an endurance phase, a speed phase, etc. In the world of strength and conditioning, there are a lot of theories and disagreements related to the concept of periodization. I will spare you the details and get to the point. There are a few reasons why coaches use periodization including peaking for competition, but the main reason is that you can only improve one attribute at a time in advanced athletes. During an endurance phase for example, they will aim to improve endurance while maintaining speed and strength.

Of course, if you don't work out at all, you can become faster, stronger, and leaner, all at the same time. But, with professional athletes this is impossible without performance enhancing drugs. So how does this apply to life? If you want to improve you have to concentrate on one or two attributes at a time, while maintaining your other qualities.

If you are drastically underperforming in life, the equivalent of a couch potato in sports, you can probably improve your career, experiences, relationships, finances, all at the same time. But, if you are already reasonably functional you will need to apply the same technique as professional athletes, focus on one thing and maintain everything else.

Picture Where you will be in Five Years after making one of two choices. Here are your possibilities.

1. Work at a normal job with normal hours and live the standard work-life balance. Live a moderate life where you experience new things, read books, exercise, and generally do things that are associated with well-adjusted people.

2. Choose an aspect of your life and focus on it. Yes, you will want to maintain everything else as much as possible, but use these 5 years to reach epic levels in this one part of your life. Make as much money as possible, Travel the world, become a black belt in a martial art etc.

Next think about which of these two options you could realistically do. If you choose option one would you really be the healthy balanced person I described? If you choose option two would you actually follow through and commit to the lifestyle? Would you be able to maintain the other aspects of your life at the same time?

Finally, which option would leave you in a better place after five years? I have experienced tremendous benefits from choosing option two, but plenty of people choose option one and live a happy satisfying life. In the rest of this book I focus on the experience phase specifically, possibly the phase which I understand the best.

5
The Benefits of an Experience Phase

Life is just a series of moments... In a sense it is always the present moment: in the past it was the present and in the future it will soon become the present. So all that really matters is the present. If you aren't appreciating this current present moment for what it is, the flow of reading, comparing your own ideas with mine, something is wrong. It's not so much that you need to be happy every single moment, I believe that this is impossible. But more importantly we should all remember to be grateful for the present moment, because that is all we have.

New experiences should be enjoyed for what they are, they are valuable in and of themselves. They don't actually have to benefit you in any way, just appreciate them as is.

But, of course, all this silly talk isn't going to convince more serious pragmatic people who want results! I will explain the potential benefits of an experience phase, based on the results from my own personal experience phase and also based on other people who have done something similar.

You Will Become more Courageous

Whenever you have a new experience there are always unknowns, sometimes these unknowns are terrifying. I remember the way I felt before I started traveling, all of the unknowns were making me nervous, would it be safe? How would I find accommodation? Would I have enough money to keep traveling? Would I miss home? Fortunately, I saw the fear correctly. Some people see fear and avoid whatever they are scared of, but usually fear is a sign that you should actually go in that direction.

When you live through an experience phase you will have the opportunity to conquer all kinds of different fears. I am not sure that it is possible to eliminate fear and anxiety altogether, but you can certainly become more courageous. Actually, you don't want to eliminate fear entirely because fear is sometimes appropriate. But, when you are more courageous you can ignore or listen to your fear depending on logic and contemplation rather than irrational reactionary thinking.

The Allegory of the Cave

The Greek Philosopher Plato introduced the concept of the Allegory of the Cave in his classic book *The Republic* around 380 BC. He used the allegory to illustrate the importance of education. Plato employs the example of a group of people who have been chained since birth in such a way that they can only stare directly forward at a wall, a fire burns in the background and it creates shadows on the wall. The prisoners have been bound so they can't move their heads and as a result they believe that the shadows are the limits of reality. They don't see anything else for their entire lives until one day they escape from their chains and they are able roam about and exit the cave.

There is a similar phenomenon whenever you try something new, you are able to see it in a new way. Before having a particular experience it is impossible to fully understand that experience. Having an experience phase will allow you to escape from your chains and understand life at a deeper level.

When I travel I often pick my destination based on which country I believe will surprise me the most. There are some countries I have never visited where I think that I have a pretty decent idea of what they might be like. For example, I have never been to Vietnam, but I have been to the Philippines, Thailand, Cambodia, and a few other nearby countries. While I would love to go to Vietnam, I suspect that it wouldn't surprise me as much as if I went to a country in a part of the world I have never visited such as the Middle-east or West Africa. That's not to say that I will never visit Vietnam, but more likely I will go there for other reasons. I know that it will be a beautiful country and a great place to stay for a few months.

When I first visited Africa I had already been traveling for 2 years. I decided that I wanted to visit Sub-Saharan Africa because I had no idea what it is was going to be like. After traveling around East Africa without a tour guide I now realize that I was right, there is no way to know what it is like without actually going there. I broke free from my chains and saw the truth just like the prisoners in Plato's story. Yes, this is a bit melodramatic, but if there is an experience you want to have, there is no way to know what it is really like until you actually do it.

Charisma and Social Skills

People who have gone through an experience phase tend to improve their charisma quite a bit. There are a number of different reasons why. One simple reason is that you will become more confident, usually confident people are magnetic and charming. When you overcome your fears and literally live out your dreams confidence is inevitable. During an experience phase you will not only overcome your larger fears, but you will also overcome many mini-insecurities. For example, some people don't like sharing things about themselves, but after an experience phase most people will probably become much more comfortable with this.

Another reason why you will experience an improvement in your charisma is that you will have a lot more stories to tell. Sure people who tell stories all the time can get a bit annoying, but you will also be able to engage with other people's stories more easily because you will be able to connect it to your own life. In general, your broader life experience will allow you to connect to a broader number of people.

Typically, but not always, you will meet a lot of people during your experience phase. During my 5 year experience period I met more different people and also a much broader range of people than the rest of my life combined. Before my experience phase I had a very narrow group of close friends, after my experience phase I now have friends from all different walks of life.

Also, think about it from this perspective: who would you rather be friends with, the guy who has lived a more balanced moderate life or the guy who spent 8 years living life to the fullest.

You will Save Money on your Experiences

This might not make sense at first, how on earth could an experience phase save you money? Don't you actually spend money on your experiences? First, I will admit that if you aren't extremely careful you will probably lose some money on an experience phase or at least not save any. But, you will save on a per experience basis.

Let's say for this example that your big dream is to surf at an advanced level. If you are living an ordinary life with normal vacation time and a typical work week, you might only get a few weeks off every year. Let's say you go on a 3 week surf vacation every year and you spend the rest of your vacation time with family. You actually end up spending a lot of money during those three weeks because you have to fly to the destination, get a hotel, rent gear, buy restaurant food etc. Also, it will take you years to get really good at surfing if you are only able to practice 3 weeks per year.

On the other hand, if you are in an experience phase, you could spend 6 months at a surf destination, buy gear, rent an apartment, cook food for yourself, and enjoy your life. You will get way more practice surfing, certainly save a lot of money per day surfing, and will have time later in your experience phase to learn more skills or even just do more surfing.

Here are your options:

1. Work a normal job with a "healthy work life balance" and spend the majority of your extra money on short surfing vacations.

2. Alternatively you take an insanely demanding job with a short term contract, ideally this job would cover your food and accommodation as well. If you work for 6 months at a job which weaker people think is "inhumane working conditions", you can surf for a year or more and have money left over.

Wisdom

Wisdom results from contemplation and experience. This is why older people are usually wiser than younger people, they have simply had more experiences and had more time to think. If you are young I'm not saying that you will instantly be wise after an experience phase, but it will certainly contribute to your wisdom as you age. A 20 year old who has a 7 year experience phase won't necessarily become a very wise 27 year old, but she will be much wiser as an older woman. The wisdom you gain from an experience phase probably won't pan out for decades, until you have had sufficient time to integrate everything you learned. In this sense, an experience phase is a very long-term investment.

Wisdom is one of the only qualities which continues to improve in old age. Based on my observations, learning ability peaks anywhere from 10-35, decision making peaks between 40-60, physical ability peaks between 15-50, but wisdom continues to increase until senility kicks in.

Self-Discovery

Try out a bunch of different things and find out what you like and what you are good at. There is a common debate in psychology on which is more important, talent or hard work. In my opinion, they are missing out on the most important factor, self-knowledge. The reality is that **everyone is naturally gifted at something**, but if you focus your hard work onto something in which you are naturally inferior at you will never achieve excellence no matter how hard you work. It's not so much a matter of are you talented or not, it's actually about finding the thing(s) you are talented at and then implementing a hard work strategy from there.

Imagine Mozart had never discovered music or imagine Newton had never learned to appreciate math/physics. Newton spent countless years working on alchemy and doing other strange experiments like putting a needle in his eye just to see what would happen. If Newton had never discovered math or physics he might have just been some unknown eccentric person from the 17th century.

When you take on an experience phase you get the chance to try all kinds of different things, hopefully in the process you will get a better idea of what you like and what you are good at. Some people get lucky and find their talent at a young age and others don't realize it until they are much older.

Die with no Regrets

Early on in my travel experiences I met an elderly German man who had been traveling the world for more than 40 years, he had been to 192 countries and had all kinds of amazing stories. I asked him a lot of questions about his life and about the countries he had visited. During our conversations he said something that really struck me "I will die with no regrets".

Over the course of my experience phase I gradually started to feel the same way, if I were to die tomorrow I would be satisfied with my life. It is a strange feeling, it's not necessarily a good feeling, but it is certainly liberating. I'm not saying that I wouldn't be disappointed if I found out I was going to die tomorrow, in fact I still have things that I want to do with my life. But, after this experience phase I feel like I could accept death more easily, certainly I am more prepared than ever for the inevitability.

People are much more likely to regret the things they never did rather than the mistakes that they made. If you commit to an experience phase you might make a few mistakes, but you will always be happy that you took the time to do the things you really wanted to do. Think back on your own life, how much would someone need to pay you to take your best experiences away from you.

The days are long, but the decades are short. I am in my late 20s now, but I know that I will be 40 before I know it and once I am 40 it won't be long until I am 50. No matter how old you are, this rule still applies. If you don't make your dreams happen, they will never happen and the time will fly by faster than you can imagine.

Increases in Creativity

What is Creativity anyway? That is a whole book in itself. Psychologists measure creativity with divergent thinking tests, this is where you take one thing and see how many other things you can relate it to. A classic divergent thinking test is "how many different things can you do with a pencil?" Valid answers would include draw, use it as a weapon, wear it as jewelry, get an object out from under a cupboard, scratch your back etc. However, psychologists and everyone else can easily see that this is an incomplete way to measure creativity. Personally, I wonder if it even makes sense to talk about general creativity. Someone could be really creative with the piano, but not be creative at all with painting.

But, one thing about creativity seems to be clear, it relies on a certain degree of inspiration. Naturally, a broad set of life experiences is a perfect source of inspiration. Some artists are able to draw inspiration from more trivial things and others seem to be able to muster up inspiration out of nowhere, but for mere mortals it makes sense to have an enormous breadth of experiences to draw upon.

You will Live Longer

Not literally, but it turns out that time perception in the human brain is very subjective. When you have a lot of new experiences you literally perceive those experiences as taking up more subjective time, while on the other hand if you do the same thing every single day the time will seemingly pass by more quickly.

David Eagleman, a neuroscience professor at Stanford University, studies the psychology and neuroscience behind time perception. He coined a term Brain Time, which highlights the subjective and variable nature of time. Have you ever had a terrifying high adrenaline experience where time seemed to slow down? Have you noticed how if you drive the same way to work every day the drive seems to fly by without you even noticing? Have you noticed how time seems to go faster and faster as you get older? Time perception depends on how much "stuff" is going on in your brain. When you do something that you have already done hundreds or thousands of times not much is being encoded and as a result time passes much more quickly, but if you are doing something new then new information is encoded into your brain and time passes by more slowly.

Eagleman recommends introducing novelty into your life by doing things like wearing your watch on your other wrist, taking a different route home every day, or rearranging your desk. Life transforming experiences will have an even more profound effect. If I think back to some of the more eventful periods during my own experience phase, months feel like years in my mind, but if I think back to some of the more repetitive points in my life, years actually feel like months. I am currently traveling in Peru with a friend of mine from Canada. It is mid-January and he just told me that it feels like it has been six months since Christmas time even though in actuality it has been less than a month.

Dealing with Change

Right now the world is changing faster than ever, it seems like it will continue to change at a faster and faster rate. In order to succeed at almost anything we have to learn to adapt.

Many industries, especially in technology, are completely transformed every couple of years. The good thing about an experience phase is that you will get very used to doing new things, naturally this will make you more comfortable dealing with change.

Even outside of business learning to deal with change is important. Personal relationships can go south or they can change. Sometimes the people closest to us change when we least expect it, we may have no choice but to adapt ourselves. Culture is changing as well, no matter what you feel about the cultural transformation you will have to find your place within it. Since I have spent so much time outside of Canada I can see how quickly Canadian culture is changing, every time I go back to my country I notice dramatic shifts in people's attitudes and philosophies. Having an experience phase will broaden your perspective and help you out in terms of dealing with the rapid shifts in the modern world.

Find Resources and also Darkness within yourself that you never knew existed

Just over four years ago, I was hiking in a rural area outside the small town of Samaipata, Bolivia. I had been hiking around all day and was on my way home. Out of the corner of my eye I saw a dog in a farmer's field, then I realized that there were actually 5 more dogs. The first dog started barking at me and it ran up to the edge of the trail, I ignored it and made sure not to look at it directly (usually this works with aggressive dogs). But, the first dog decided to charge me and the others followed suit.

In some countries we are used to a different kind of dog, but in countries like Bolivia, especially in the rural areas, the dogs aren't what you find in a Canadian suburb. They are savage, unneutered, territorial and used to violence. When the dogs attacked I was shocked and terrified, I thought they were going to kill me, there is no way I could fight off 6 big dogs. Somehow I made the right decision, I reached down and picked up a rock. As soon as I put my hand in the air to throw it, the dogs scattered. Dogs in a lot of developing countries are used to people throwing rocks at them and they hate it. After this event, and a few other similar events during my experience phase I realized that when I am physically threatened I respond quickly and effectively. This has made me much more confident in dangerous situations.

Ok now my capacity for darkness. When I was four years old I found out that farmers have to kill animals before selling them as meat, after this I told my parents that I wanted to be a vegetarian. As an adult I am amazed at how supportive my parents were. We stopped eating meat entirely. Briefly, we followed a diet where we only ate food that would naturally fall from a plant e.g. fruit, nuts, seeds. That didn't last long, but we continued to follow a vegetarian diet until I was about 13 and then we followed a pescetarian diet.

Later on in my teens I started experimenting with eating meat. When I moved away for University I gradually started eating more and more meat. Eventually I started eating meat at every single meal. I never fully dealt with this at an ethical level, I just started eating meat and that was that. I always felt that it would be more ethical to hunt or at least kill the animal myself, but I never did anything about it. In Uganda I bought and killed my first chicken and in Ethiopia I bought and killed my first sheep, both times I killed the animal with a knife and with help from people who had done it before. Here's where the darkness comes out. There was no regret or remorse at all, in fact it was an exhilarating experience. It felt natural, fascinating, and straightforward. I am not normally very good with my hands, in fact I don't like fixing cars, doing physical art, or building things, I spend a lot more time in my head. But, killing and cleaning the chickens and sheep actually came very naturally to me.

In understanding this darkness I understand my own primitive predatory nature more deeply. I have come to terms with that reality. Does that mean I can't move past my own base instincts? Of course not, one day I might even consider going back to being a vegetarian (or even a vegan). I will need to do more research and understand the ethical implications more deeply. I might also keep my omnivorous diet and take up hunting as a hobby. Ultimately, my experience has broadened my perspective.

If you put yourself into a new situation you will find new resources within yourself and you will realize that you can do so much more than you previously believed. Will you find a dark side that you didn't know about? I'm not sure, but I can guarantee that you will learn something about yourself if you push out of your comfort zone.

6
Is It for Everyone?

Nope, not everyone wants an experience phase, and many people don't need an experience phase either. People are different and we are all meant to take on very different roles. Part of what makes humans so unique is that we cooperate and specialize. Our societies function because people master certain skills. One person specializes in dentistry, another specializes in fixing cars, another person designs houses. It is a mark of immaturity when someone tries to get everyone else to be exactly like them. Since I have had an amazing experience phase in my own life, it is tempting to try to convince other people to do the same, but I won't. Unless, of course, I think that they also have the temperament and motivation to do it.

Interestingly, **human beings mostly differ quantitatively instead of qualitatively**. What this means is that we all share the same fundamental qualities, but differ in terms of how much we express them. This applies biologically as well as psychologically. We all have the same cell structure, the same organs, and the same kinds of tissue in our body. We all have more or less the same number of bones and the same bone structure.

Some people have longer femurs and as a result they are taller. On the other hand, some people have shorter humerus bones and so their arms are shorter. While there are certainly genetic anomalies, these are the exception. Even genetic anomalies follow the general human patterns in every aspect except for their specific anomaly (e.g. someone with 6 fingers is qualitatively normal in nearly every other way).

The same thing goes for psychological variables. We all have varying degrees of excitement, extroversion, openness, intelligence, fear, neuroticism, need for novelty, etc. Everyone experiences or displays all of these variables to some extent. Just like physical anomalies, there are also psychological genetic anomalies. But, these are very rare. The differences in people stem more from how much they express these different qualities rather than whether or not they apply at all.

Big Five Personality Traits

It's irresponsible to talk about personality without bringing up the Big Five. As you might expect, the Big Five is split up into five different components. One of these components is openness to new experience. I listed the characteristics that make up openness earlier, but I think they are worth repeating.

- Desire for Novelty
- Interest in Art
- Creativity
- Intellectual Curiosity
- Imagination
- Aesthetic Sensitivity

If you score high on openness to new experience this is another strong sign that you should consider an experience phase. People who score very high on openness to new experience or very high on experience seeking, but are never able to live out their dreams, will probably regret it for their entire lives.

One question to ask is whether you would be satisfied living out your entire life never actually having those experiences that you dream about. Chances are that if you don't have an experience phase you won't ever actually live out your dreams. You might get to live some of them, but most of the time life gets in the way.

Do You Have an Adventurous Spirit?

This one might seem pretty straightforward but I think that the question is a bit deeper than it might appear on the surface. Some people have a strong need for adventure, but don't naturally find themselves in adventurous situations. That was me, I really wanted to go on big adventures but if I didn't force myself to do something I would just stay inside of my room all day. I had to intentionally create a habit of going out and pursuing adventure, otherwise adventure wouldn't come to me.

I think some people on the other hand find that adventure comes naturally to them. These people might have close friends who like to do fun stuff or maybe they just have a level of natural energy which fuels them to go do things. So even if you aren't this typical "adventurous type", you might still have an adventurous spirit, you just need to be intentional about bringing it out. Some people don't have an adventurous spirit at all. Probably they don't need to have an experience phase, at least not a very long one.

Another question to ask is whether or not you are the kind of person who needs to do things in reality, or whether you are happy imagining. Personally I enjoy watching movies, reading novels, and learning about historical adventures. But, when I take in this information I start thinking about doing it myself, I'm not satisfied watching someone else. Some people don't have to go to an ashram in India, they are perfectly happy reading about someone else's experiences. There's nothing wrong with people who don't have the adventurous spirit. What's wrong is when an adventurous person gets their dreams stifled.

I had one random conversation with a hotel owner in Bolivia. He was born on Isla Del Sol on Lago Titicaca near the Peruvian border. The man was illiterate and not very curious about the world. He had only ever been to one other place in his entire life which was a town called Copacabana a 45 minute boat ride away. He had never even been to Peru 12 kilometers away from Copacabana or to the capital city of Bolivia, La Paz which is 150 kilometers away from Copacabana. He had no desire to visit these other places, in fact, he was perfectly satisfied managing his hotel and tending to his plants.

If I had been in his shoes I would have been enormously curious about other places. No this isn't just a matter of him not knowing the possibilities, he knew all about La Paz, Peru, etc. Instead it is a matter of temperament. If you don't have a personal call to adventure don't feel pressured to have an experience phase.

The conversation I had with this man in Bolivia is stuck in my memory as a constant reminder that people are very different. Some people need extreme stimulation and are very curious about the world, other people prefer a more ordered organized life. This conversation made it very clear to me that not everyone needs an experience phase.

Is your Life Stagnant?

Another factor is whether or not your life is stagnant, i.e. you are in a rut. Most people have had at least one period in their life where nothing improves. Maybe things even get worse. Here are some signs that your life is stagnant.

- You aren't saving at least 10% of your yearly salary.
- You aren't progressing in your career.
- You aren't trying new things.
- You aren't improving your health, fitness, or relationships.
- You aren't learning new things.
- You aren't developing spiritually.

The main concept behind a dedicated phase is that you focus your energy into developing one of these aspects of your life while maintaining or at least almost maintaining the others. Some people are able to improve on all of them at once, but I believe that most people need to focus. If most or all of those previous statements are true you are in a rut. And one excellent way to get out of a rut is to have an experience phase. On the other hand, if you are performing well on most of these factors an experience phase might be a bad idea "if it ain't broke don't fix it". An experience phase will change you dramatically and you might not end up in a better situation.

You don't need to be Rich

Which stage are you at in your career? Here is a mistake that many young people make. They are working a low-paying go-nowhere job, but they feel like they need to earn more money to have an experience phase. The idea is that the experience phase is expensive and they don't earn enough to pull it off. This the wrong approach. When they are earning good money, especially when they are at their highest earning potential, that is the worst time to have an experience phase. Actually, at their highest earning point is when they should be concentrating on their work. The best time to have an experience phase is when you aren't earning much money and you aren't progressing in your career.

Some people will think "how can you have an experience phase without already being rich?" Maybe this question sounds silly to you, it sounds absurd to me. I have met so many people who have had experience phases in their life without much money at all. However, I do think that a lot of people have a reasoning pattern similar to this. Of course, it does depend in part on how expensive your dreams really are. Chances are you have a lot of different dreams, some of which are very affordable. Either way, it is usually much easier to find a way to be frugal and creative in order to make your dreams cheaper, instead of earning the money required to live them out lavishly.

So the question is: "are you playing a high stakes game at work". Meaning if high performance means high reward in terms of money or career advancement you know that you are at the wrong point in your life for an experience phase.

Another consideration is **your family/cultural environment**. I come from a family and a culture where people are encouraged to pursue their own life paths. My parents would teach me lessons and give suggestions, but as an adult everything is up to me. Sure they weren't happy with every decision I made, but at least it isn't a cultural taboo to pursue my own path. The same goes for my friends and extended family, most people encouraged my desire to live my own way.

Some people come from a very different culture or family where pursuing your own dreams is considered selfish or even considered to be a form of betrayal. While I certainly advocate following your own path in life, it is also important to maintain your relationships with your family. If you feel like you will permanently damage your familial relationships by going into an experience phase consider not doing it.

Next **consider the actual experiences that you want to have**. Can they be done in your current city/town or will you need to go somewhere else to do them? One big advantage of the experience phase is that it is easier to actually travel to the best destination to have a specific experience. Another question is how much commitment will your experiences need. Do you want to learn to play the guitar or do you actually want to start a band and play live performances? Do you want to learn salsa dancing or do you want to travel to Colombia? Are you happy going surfing once a year on holiday or do you want to live in a beach town and go surfing every single day? Do you want to practice meditation every day or do you want to live in an ashram for a few months?

These questions should help you decide whether or not your experiences can be had on the side or whether they will need a focused experience phase. If you are satisfied learning to play the guitar at home using YouTube or going to salsa classes two times per week, you really don't need to have an experience phase at all.

Your value system is very important as well. When you undertake an experience phase you end up sacrificing stability. When you try all kinds of new things and get out of your comfort zone you don't know what is going to happen, it is stepping out into the unknown.

Some people have a strong need for stability and a predictable future. Normally, you also put other parts of your life on hold like family, career, community etc. Are your experiences worth sacrificing your stability? Are your experiences so valuable that you are willing to take a break from other goals in your life? For me personally, experiences have been very important in my own value system, perhaps the most important thing. But, many people would rather have a stable career than a bunch of experiences which don't actually provide value on their own.

Face your Problems Head on

If you are deciding whether or not to have an experience phase you need to figure out if you are running from your problems or running towards your problems. The right way to live life is to run towards problems, no I am not saying that you need to create problems, instead you should address your problems head on. For example, let's say that you are out of shape, but your situation isn't that bad, in fact it isn't inconveniencing you at all except when you do some kind of physical activity. You have two options.

1. You ignore the problem and let your fitness deteriorate over time.
2. You start addressing your fitness right now.

Option 2 is running to your problems and option 1 is running from your problems. What happens if you choose option 1 and neglect your ailing fitness? Eventually it will catch up on and you will have to address it. But, you don't get to decide the terms, you will just have to deal with the reality that nature hands you. Sure, if you start addressing your fitness right now you will still have to face the problem, but instead you get to face it on your own terms. You get to choose what time of day you workout, which days you workout, even what kind of workout you do. You could lift weights, do yoga, play squash, start hiking etc. If you wait until you have a problem you might be so broken that you end up only having a few options for your workout routine (e.g. physio).

Money is another perfect example. You could save money right now or you could ignore your finances until you need to retire or have some big bill to pay. If you start saving right away you will be able to budget and choose what you purchase vs. what you don't purchase. You will be able to address the problem while more or less maintaining the lifestyle you want to lead. On the other hand, let's say you wait until your finances become a problem, you won't have that luxury. You might have to drastically reduce your spending at some random time in your life when you least expect it.

So when you are considering an experience phase it is vital to understand which you are doing. Are on the hunt for your insecurities? Are you out trying to expand your comfort zone? Or are you trying to avoid some other problem in your life? The point of the experience phase is to improve yourself and live life to the fullest, not a way to avoid getting hard work done.

Risk and the Experience Phase

How risky are the experiences you want to have? And will your experiences harm anyone else? Do you want to travel to Southeast Asia and live on the beach for a few months? Learn Judo in Japan? Hike the Appalachian Trail? These are all fairly low risk experiences.

I am fortunate in that the majority of the experiences I always wanted to have were relatively low-risk. There was one very high-risk experiences I never followed through with. When I was a teenager I was obsessed with mixed martial arts, I knew all the fighter's styles, records, and would wait eagerly months before a big fight. I always wanted to compete, I probably fantasized about competing multiple times a day for most of my teen years. The funny thing is that I barely ever trained, except for a punching bag in our family garage. The issue is that I didn't just want to have one fight, I wanted to fight professionally. Fortunately, I never followed through with this dream, naturally competing in fighting is extremely risky. I can remember when I was 16 I had decided that I was going to train in a mma school and follow through with my goal. Pretty soon afterwards I tore my ACL playing soccer. When I realized I couldn't train I was upset for months. While at the time it felt terrible, the ACL tear was a blessing in disguise for many reasons.

Before deciding that you want to have an experience phase decide whether or not the risk is worth it. By taking on an experience phase you aren't suddenly immune to dangers. In fact, whatever injuries, illnesses, or financial damage you take on during your experience phase could stay with you forever.

Imagine three separate life paths over the next 5 years.

1. An Experience Phase.
2. A General phase (do everything)
3. Another dedicated phase

Think about where you will be after 5 years of pursuing any of these life paths. Which person would you rather be after 5 years?

New Experiences don't make you Happy

Many people are aware of the Buddhist idea that material objects won't bring you happiness because you will always want more and more. In this philosophy the wanting itself is suffering, but once you get the material object it doesn't provide relief. You can actually apply the same principle to experiences. Experiences don't make you happy and the constant pursuit of experiences doesn't make you happy either. There will never be a point where you say "that experience changed me in such a fundamental way that I now know how to be happy forever." The joy we get from experiences is just as fleeting as the joy we get from material objects.

Don't expect the experience itself to give you joy, rather joy will come throughout the journey. The wanting will bring suffering, but it also brings joy at the same time.

Many people have a strong need for a sense of progress, in fact I am the same way. If you are this type of person you may find the experience phase frustrating because it won't feel like you are making any kind of progress. Actually this kind of personality usually imbues a sense of progress onto their experiences, but normally this sense of progress is irrational, it is simply a way to deal with a need.

A perfect example is through my meditation. My brain would often create a story where my meditation was somehow progressing from lower to higher levels, but in reality it was probably changing in a much more random way. I still appreciate all of the experiences that I had meditating and I think that they have informed many aspects of my life, but I suspect that I could have had those experiences in many different orders, there was no hierarchy. So if you have the kind of mind that tends to group things into stages, progressions, hierarchies, you will probably find yourself doing the same thing with your experiences.

Potentially it will be frustrating and/or enlightening as you discover that there isn't much progression to your experiences, rather there is simply a lot of randomness. While I don't think that a strong desire to progress will actually hinder your experience phase, it might make the experience phase less pleasant. If you are this kind of person with a high need for progress understand that some people are on the opposite end of the spectrum, they are able to move from experience to experience without much need to feel like they are progressing towards something.

The exception would be experiences which literally have a skill component. E.g. surfing, martial arts, chess, sculpting, trekking etc. If you practice any skill you will get better at it.

Maslow's Hierarchy of Needs

The psychologist Abraham Maslow created a hierarchy of life phases in 1954. Many people intuitively agree with his ideas whether they are familiar with them or not. The concept is that throughout your life your priorities change based on whether or not you have achieved certain stages. I actually think that in his original publication he was fundamentally wrong in his theory. People are constantly jumping around between his different stages and there is certainly no need to finish a stage to move onto the next. I believe that Maslow's theory is important because his mistake perfectly illustrates the mistake that many people make in their lives. First, let me highlight his original model, when he first published the idea in 1954 there were five separate stages.

1. The Physiological Stage: Food, Sex, Sleep, Water, Shelter

2. Safety: Personality Security, Financial Security, Emotional Security

3. Love/Belonging: Friendships, Intimacy, Family

4. Esteem/Ego - lower version: status, fame, prestige - higher version: competence, master, independence

5. Self-Actualization (later on Maslow changed this to transcendence): mate acquisition, parenting, utilizing abilities, talents, pursuing a goal, seeking happiness.

Many people create a similar model in their own minds or they see this theory and think that it is very logical. If you don't have food how can you even think about being happy or becoming more competent at something? It seems like the whole idea makes sense, you have to progress from each stage to the next. Note: According to Maslow this is how people actually live their lives, it isn't necessarily a prescription for what is the best way to live your life. But, I think that an important concept underlying his idea is that if you are aware of this model you can consciously progress through each stage and eventually self-actualize.

Here is my problem with the theory. Many people jump between stages all the time. For example, some monks will intentionally give up physiological needs like food, sex, or shelter to achieve spiritual enlightenment. They will also give up on their friendships, security, and their ego. The way I see it, spiritual enlightenment is an excellent form of self-actualization or transcendence. Monks in all kinds of religious traditions skip the other phases in order to self-actualize. Sure in some traditions monks will live together in big groups which helps achieve safety, friendships, family, and other stages, but in other traditions monks will go off into the wilderness on their own.

Another example is mate acquisition. Many people find their long-term partner and then move through life together, achieving the other stages as a team. Or some people master a skill, but are complete hermits and don't have any connections to friends/family. There is no reason to believe that you need to progress through these stages. In fact, you can skip all the way to the highest stage Self-actualization and then you can go back and take care of the more "primitive" phases. Whichever order that works for you is fine.

The mistake a lot of people make is they feel like they have to get all of their ducks in a row before they can self-actualize, the reality is that you can start self-actualizing right now.

And by the way, self-actualizing isn't an end point. There is no time in your life where you are "self-actualized" and you reach enlightenment. That is a myth that self-progressed gurus create to earn followers. Self-actualization is a never-ending process where you are constantly working to stay on the right path. Throughout the course of your life you will constantly interact with all 5 stages, you never completely graduate from any of the stages.

Responsibilities

In addition to personality there are other important life considerations. Particularly responsibilities. Responsibility is a factor which varies enormously across people. On the one end you have single people without children working go-nowhere jobs (or even unemployed) and on the other end you have parents or people who hold important positions in government/business. People who have important responsibilities normally shouldn't take on an experience phase. Imagine a father of three young children decides to dedicate himself to pursuing his dreams. So he quits his job, moves to Hollywood and tries his luck as a professional actor. Sounds like a recipe for a disaster.

Just to be clear I am certainly not saying that he shouldn't try new things or even that he can't ever have an experience phase. I am just saying not to have an experience phase right now, he can try new things on the side when he has free time.

It is important to note that some people do find ways to balance a lot of responsibility with an experience phase. The best and most common examples are parents who travel the world with their children. I even know of single parents who have traveled extensively with very young kids. I can't recommend everyone does this simply because many families don't have stability or desire to pull it off, however some families are certainly capable of traveling the world successfully.

Also, many people have experience phases when their kids leave the home. So people with a lot of responsibility can (and maybe should) have an experience phase, but they may want to prioritize other parts of their life first.

Are you Antifragile?

Nassim Nicholas Taleb developed a concept called antifragility, or rather you could say that he cleverly explained something fairly obvious which most people hadn't noticed. What is the opposite of fragile? Something very sturdy right? Actually no. When you apply pressure to something fragile it breaks. When you apply pressure to something sturdy what happens? Nothing. That's not the opposite of breaking. The opposite of breaking would be getting stronger. So antifragility is distinct from sturdiness.

An example of antifragility would be a muscle, when you apply pressure to a muscle it gets stronger. In fact, all biological systems have antifragile processes, this includes human psychology (whatever doesn't kill you only makes you stronger). When you undertake an experience phase you will likely have some psychologically damaging experiences, this is inevitable when you take risks. The question is will these damaging experiences traumatize you or strengthen you? Is your personality fragile, sturdy, or antifragile? Of course it depends on the situation, but the goal is to become as antifragile as possible.

Negative uncomfortable experiences are almost inevitable in a properly executed experience phase. If you know how to respond to negative experiences with antifragility you will get more out of your experience phase.

Do you gain Momentum?

Another thing to ask yourself if you are considering any kind of dedicated phase is whether or not you have the kind of personality that gains momentum. Some people like to focus on one or two things because they gain momentum over time, basically the more they do it the more they enjoy it and the better they get at it. When I am working hard for a period of a few months I tend to enjoy my work more the more I do it. When I was having my experience phase, traveling the world and meeting tons of people I gained momentum over time.

Some people are the opposite, they like to have more breaks and balance in their life. These kinds of people tend to dislike things that they do all the time, they might not enjoy having a new experience every single day, instead they might enjoy having a new experience every second weekend. When I am not in an experience phase it is hard for me to put in the effort to go have a new experience, but when I was in my experience phase it was almost effortless. I just got into that mode of operation and ran with it.

***

Life is often a balance of going with the flow and living intentionally. If you try to control everything all the time you will miss out on all kinds of opportunities due to closed-mindedness, but if you never live intentionally you might get swept down current on a river you shouldn't be in.

Balancing the Factors and making your Decision

I included a lot of different considerations for deciding whether or not an experience phase is right for you. It might feel like too much to deal with, but all of the data is useful. Yes, it is too much for your conscious mind, but not too much for your subconscious. When there are too many different factors to consider, then you should use your gut to solve the problem. Don't try to use an organized system for balancing every single consideration, rather learn to listen to your instinct.

When deciding whether to have an experience phase make sure that all of the following are in order. You should be...

1. Emotionally stable
2. Thinking rationally
3. In a contemplative state of mind.

You don't want to commit to an experience phase when you are thinking poorly or feeling unstable. This is an important decision and it should be made when you are at your best. Not as a reaction to another event in your life. You want to be rational enough to evaluate the decision with a clear ahead. If you aren't in the right state of mind when you make the decision you might commit yourself to an experience phase when it isn't actually appropriate. Or you might choose the incorrect length of time for your experience phase.

You might say that it doesn't matter if you decide on an experience phase during an emotionally unstable state because you can simply change your mind later. If you commit to an experience phase in your own mind and you don't follow through with it, this isn't truly living intentionally. Inevitably you will reach points where you don't feel like following through, but the idea behind living intentionally is making your decisions in a rational state of mind and then following through with that decision even if you don't want to do it later.

You want to develop a pattern of always following through with the commitments that you make to yourself, every time you follow through with a commitment you strengthen this pattern and every time you break a commitment you weaken this pattern. Understand that committing to an experience phase is a serious matter and don't commit to doing it until you are sure that it is the right decision.

7
When to Start?

The natural inclination is to say that the best time to start an experience phase is when you are young and the younger you are the better, but I believe it is more complicated than this. Actually, a lot of people have an experience phase when they retire and their children have left the home. There are all kinds of sensible times to have an experience phase, but there are also some terrible times as well.

An example of a bad time to have an experience phase is when you have a lot of important responsibilities. This is when you have children or other dependents. Another example would be when you have an important job or role in an organization. If you decide to commit to an experience phase when you have substantial responsibilities you will likely underperform. It's much better to wait however many years are necessary to be in a state of fewer responsibilities.

Another bad time to take on an experience phase is when you are playing a high stakes game in your life. Meaning that if you perform well you will be able to reap high rewards, but if you perform poorly you either won't get these rewards or maybe you will even lose resources. One example of a high stakes game is a computer programmer who is working for a successful start-up. At this point in the company's development it is absolutely vital for the employees to concentrate as much of their energy onto their work as possible, if the programmer decides to have an experience phase this will be bad for the company and will potentially damage his long-term career prospects.

Don't take on an experience phase when you are simply bored with your regular life. In many ways boredom isn't a bad thing and it isn't something to shy away from. Rather, boredom is something to experience and to learn from. If you are constantly feeling bored consider taking on something that requires a lot of focus and effort, don't try to get rid of your boredom by going out and having a bunch of different experiences. The experience phase is never a cure for boredom, it is about giving yourself the time and focus to live out your dreams. Having an experience phase certainly won't cure boredom, if anything it might exacerbate it.

***

Some young people believe that they should wait to commit to an experience phase until they are earning a lot of money and have sufficient financial resources. Actually, this is the wrong approach. The absolute worst time to take on an experience phase is when you are at your peak earnings. At this point you should be doubling down on your finances and trying to earn/save as much as possible. Younger people who don't have any money are actually at the perfect point in their lives to have an experience phase.

Never had a fulltime job, never lived alone (18-25):

This is the period of life right after high school. Ideally people going through this phase get a lot of new life experiences whether they are going through an experience phase or not. They might get their first fulltime job, graduate from University, and/or get their own apartment.

It might seem like a logical time to have an experience phase. After all, at this time, they have nothing to lose. Normally no responsibilities and normally not very many belongings. They are almost unemployable and most people in this period don't know much about themselves or what they want to be doing with their lives. These are all strong reasons to have an experience phase right after high school.

Now for the downsides. First off they haven't developed much wisdom yet, so an experience phase could be risky. They might get caught up in excessive partying or drug use. They might do something very dangerous which gets them into trouble. Of course some people in this period of their lives are already mature enough to keep themselves safe, but others might have problems.

Another potential downside is that they might not fully take advantage of their experience phase. An older person has a deeper understanding of the potential benefits of different experiences and can understand them in the context of the rest of their life, but a very young adult without much life experiences themselves won't necessarily understand what they should be spending their time doing.

For example, they might spend their entire experience phase partying in their hometown. Alternatively, if they had had an experience phase 5-10 years later they would likely pursue more profound experiences. The point is that when they are older they might feel like they didn't fully take advantage of their experience phase, as the expression goes "youth is wasted on the young".

My suggestion would be to take on a longer experience phase if you are going to do it at a very young age. There are two reasons why:

1. You have more time in your life to dedicate to other things.

2. You might feel like you "wasted" your first couple years in the experience phase just learning basic stuff.

I started my experience phase at 21 right when I was finishing my University Studies. This was the perfect time. Other than a few summer jobs I had never actually held a full-time job. For me personally, I didn't have a lot of life experiences outside of education or my meditation practices. Fortunately, I didn't do anything during my experience phase which caused any lasting damage.

Some Work Experience, a few years living alone, maybe some traveling or serious relationships 22-30:

Another very reasonable time to have an experience phase. At this point you will have accumulated some maturity and are ready to tackle your experience phase with a reasonable degree of caution. You will have had enough experiences already to know what you should be spending your time doing and what you shouldn't be spending your time doing.

For some people this isn't the best time to have a very long experience phase because it might interfere with their ability to have children. But, I think that if you want to have an experience phase while you are young this is the best of both worlds. You still probably don't have a lot of responsibilities (depending on the person), you probably don't own a lot of stuff, and you may still have some questions as to what you want to do with your life.

Middle of Career, possibly children, peak responsibilities, peak earnings 25+:

Probably not the best time to have an experience phase simply because you likely have other things to worry about. When you are 36 with three kids, a full-time job, and a mortgage the last thing you want to be thinking about is your dream of cycling around Europe. Yes you can still do something adventurous like this and many people do take on experience phases during their 30s or 40, my point is that it just isn't the ideal time for most people. If you are in your 30s right now and have a huge list of experiences that you want to have don't worry. A lot of people actually take on an experience phase in retirement.

The Golden Years, retirement, children move out:

I won't pretend to know anything about retirement or the best way to have a rewarding retirement. But, I have noticed that a lot of people actually have a lot interesting experiences during this part of their life. They go out and do all the things they never had a chance to do when they were younger. This is easy for me to say as a young guy, but the truth is that most of the limits we see in ourselves are actually self-imposed. Even limitations like old age can be transcended with the right mindset.

From my perspective life isn't over in old age. While some people that I know seem to give up in their 50s, I have noticed other people continue to live life to the fullest well into their 60s, 70s, and even 80s. My grandma got remarried twice in her 80s and traveled to France as well as Costa Rica. She even went ziplining hundreds of feet above the jungle canopy. Of course, physical limitations might prevent you from doing certain things, but a lot of people still manage to find a way to get over whatever physical limitations they have.

Some people see their retirement years as the time in their life when they get to finally "relax". I am young so I have not yet earned an opinion on this, but I will give my opinion anyway. There's never a point in our lives where we just stop doing things and "relax". This is accepting an early death, it is a form of emotional suicide. Relaxing is great when you need it, but spending more than a couple of days just relaxing is actually miserable. I am sure most people reading agree with me, but if you think I am wrong here is an experiment you can try.

When you have some time off work spend a week doing as little as possible, try to be as comfortable as possible. Before that week begins make sure you have food in your fridge, a clean place, plenty of movies downloaded etc. Make your life as easy as possible, do as little as possible, be as comfortable as possible. Watch what happens, chances are you will feel awful. Some people will start to get depressed, some people will get anxiety, and some people will be angry. You might feel good for a few hours and if you have a very stressful life you might even feel good for a few days, but this won't last long.

True happiness comes from accepting the fact that life is a never ending struggle. A struggle to experience new things, a struggle to earn money, and a struggle to find good relationships. Struggle is the nature of life.

Why do people have this fantasy that one day they can just take it easy and do nothing during retirement? I think that this comes from the fact that a lot of people are overstressed in their lives. They just don't feel like they get to relax enough. Their jobs are stressful and when they get home their family lives are even more stressful. So whenever they get a chance to really relax for a few hours it feels amazing. But, I think that people who pay attention to their own emotions will understand that it just isn't that pleasant to relax for days on end.

Stress is way easier to deal with during a dedicated phase because you choose the stress yourself. Much of the stress that many people deal with on a day to day basis is imposed by someone else or is imposed by life itself.

Adolescence

Some people have told me that they already had their experience phase during their adolescence. I see this as a basic misunderstanding of what an experience phase really is. During adolescence many people experiment with new personalities, fashion, rebelliousness, and other more dangerous activities. The problem is that most people actually feel trapped and unable to do what they really want to do during adolescence. In my opinion, it isn't a true experience phase because teenagers are legally, psychologically, and financially limited in terms of what they can do.

Probably the reason why so many teenagers are frustrated with their lives is that biologically and neurologically they are being primed to take on the roles of adults, but in modern society they are still effectively children. This creates a psychological messiness in their minds which compounds with the influence of their peers.

Now I am certainly not saying that teenagers should be given unlimited autonomy, that could cause a lot of dangerous social problems. I'm not even necessarily saying that teenagers should be give more autonomy than they already have. Basically, what I am saying is that most people don't get to really truly experiment during their teens. Also, an experience phase is not simply extending adolescence, it is something different entirely.

As a side note about teenagers and experience phases I have actually met two different 17 year olds traveling the world. I met one of them in Cambodia and the other in Thailand. They were both from the United States of America and they were both having the time of their lives. The 17 year old I met in Thailand was on his way to Nepal, we were sitting on a bus in Bangkok heading to the airport. He told me all about his adventures so far and was more than thrilled to recount his experiences selling drugs on one of the touristic islands off the coast of Thailand. While he was clearly getting awesome experiences he was also taking a lot of unnecessary risks.

The issue is that when you go through an experience phase it can make you so passionate about life that you start to forget the potential risks of doing something like selling drugs in Thailand. If he had waited 10 years he probably wouldn't have done something so stupid. The other 17 year old that I met seemed totally fine traveling on his own. He was staying in a hostel like everyone else and seemed to have a good head on his shoulders.

When I was 16 I kept trying to convince my parents to send me to Thailand for the summer. I like to believe that I would have made good decisions, but I am not totally sure. Either way it would have been a bad idea for me to go at the time because I wasn't earning my own money, maybe I could have saved some money working a part-time job to support my trip. My parents actually ended up sending me on a school trip to Costa Rica that summer which was very generous of them.

Here are my recommendations for teenagers who are interested in having an experience phase right after high school:

1. While you are finishing high school I suggest getting a part-time job and saving as much money as possible. The money will be helpful and the work experience will be useful when you are looking for a full-time job after high school. You don't want to rely on your parents to pay for your Experience Phase.

2. Start meditating every day. This will help you make better decisions and is an interesting experience in itself.

3. Learn how to cook some simple meals for yourself. Make sure you have at least four options which take less than 30 minutes to cook. This will make your life much easier when you are living on your own.

4. Focus on the Foundational Experiences I highlight in the following chapter.

A Trade-off

The later you have your experience phase and the older you are, the less risky it will be. You will have more experiences already which will inform you in taking sensible risks. Also, your wisdom will help you take advantage of the experience phase to the best of your ability and not waste your time with experiences that aren't actually profound. But, the older you are the more responsibilities you will probably have and the more career opportunities you will be neglecting. Also, the older you are the less time you have to spend on different phases. So basically it is always a balance between factors and there is no ideal time.

It is possible that you are comfortable in your current situation and just don't feel like having an experience phase right now, but that doesn't mean that you shouldn't have one. In fact, having an experience phase might still be a good idea if other factors in your life are in the right position. For example, if you have a natural career break. You might be eager to move onto the next stage in your career, but consider holding off. You might never get a chance to have an experience phase again.

If you don't have a good reason to not have an experience phase, then I say you should have one right now. A lot of people talk about all the different things that they want to do with their lives, but they never actually follow through. Actions speak louder than words. If you don't do it right now there is a good chance that you never will. If you are in a reasonably good position to have an experience phase, now is the right time.

I'm certainly not saying to quit your job today, at least sleep on it first. And of course you don't necessarily have to quit your job to take on an experience phase, everyone's experience phase and jobs are much different. Also, if you do have to actually quit your job, it might not be ideal to quit it right away. The experience phase starts when you start preparing. You might begin by saving money or taking some classes on the side. Normally, you don't go from no experiences to a wild round the world adventure. Most people start small and gradually ramp up their experience phase.

The most important thing is to actually do it. One worry I have writing this book is that it will give people "paralysis by analysis". Basically they will think about the problem so much that they never actually act on it. Despite being a very analytical guy, I am lucky in that I have never had a problem with "paralysis by analysis". I have plenty of other psychological challenges, but fortunately this isn't one of them. Usually the more I analyze something the more likely I am to actually do it. However, a lot of people do have this problem. If you want to have an experience phase at some point you will need to actually take the jump.

My suggestion would be to commit to the phase and start taking action. Once you start moving in the right direction you will find that everything falls into place.

It is very unlikely that you will be able to have an experience phase at the "perfect time" in your life. The chances are that you will have to make some sacrifices and those sacrifices might be very substantial. Instead the challenge will be determining whether or not this is the best time to do it, whether those sacrifices are outweighed by the potential benefits.

Where do your Challenges come from?

If you are at a stage in your life where the only challenges you face are the challenges that life dealt you, this is an indication that you should take on an experience phase. I firmly believe that people should intentionally exit their comfort zones and in the process take on new challenges regularly. There is a massive difference between overcoming challenges that fell on your lap and overcoming challenges you sought out yourself. The experience phase is just as challenging as any other phase, it isn't an excuse to be lazy for a couple of years. For some people the experience phase might even be the most challenging period of their lives.

When your life is stale and things aren't progressing in any way you know that it is time to consider an experience phase. I'm not talking about things progressing in terms of weeks or even a few months, I am talking about a situation where you don't believe that you will make any progress within a couple of years.

Scheduling your Experience Phase into your Life

Ideally you will set up your experience phase at a natural career break. This is right after high school before you have any kind career, right after University, or after finishing a big project/contract. Alternatively, in some careers it is part of the culture to have a sabbatical. Of course, not everyone's career path has natural breaks, in which case it is up to you to decide whether you want to wait until retirement or go for it while you are still working.

Ideally, you will be able to find a way to maintain your job. While I went through my experience phase I kept the same job over the course of 5 years. How did I manage this while traveling the world? I actually quit my job a total of 4 times, but every time I was lucky enough to be taken back. Eventually I negotiated a position where I would work for set contracts and then go back to traveling. However, not everyone will have this freedom.

Possibly your experience phase doesn't involve a lot of traveling and in this case you might be able to keep your job throughout. You probably won't get a lot of promotions because you will be dedicated to other things, but at least when your experience phase is over you will still be in a decent position in your career. Also, some people will be able to work online, these people can maintain their job while traveling the world.

Perhaps you already think like me. You already organize your life into different phases. Of course, when you finish a phase it is often a good idea to take on a new one. As I mentioned earlier, many people take on an experience phase after their children have moved out of the house. Personally, I took on an experience phase after dedicating myself to my intellect for 5 years.

Overall choosing the best time to have an experience phase should be based on a cost benefit analysis. Take all of the different factors into consideration. Eventually you will need to go with your gut instinct. It's impossible to logically compare all of the disparate factors like responsibilities vs. opportunities. That's like comparing apples and oranges. But, if you know how to listen to your instinct, you will be able to make a sensible decision.

8
Some Ideas for Experiences

My favorite part about the experience phase is that you can make it up as you go along. It doesn't have to be carefully planned out, unless if planning is necessary to make sure a specific experience happens. I had a list of things I really wanted to do, go to Burning Man, travel to India, Colombia, Ethiopia etc. But I didn't have a special order that I wanted to do them in.

I recommend a lot of different experiences in this chapter, some of them involve joining groups. I.E. volunteering, communes, taking classes, working abroad etc. Any time you commit to becoming a part of a group I urge you to do your research. A lot of people (including me) will flippantly say things like "you should go teach English in Korea" without specifying that it can be difficult to find the right place to work. A perfect example is ayahuasca in South America. There are all kinds of phony shamans trying to earn a quick buck by offering up ayahuasca ceremonies, sometimes they don't even give you real ayahuasca. On the other hand, if you do some research, you will be able to find the ceremonies which are more authentic. When it comes to any of my recommendations bear in mind that I always suggest doing your research before committing to something big.

In this chapter I have laid out a big list of possible experiences you might want to have at some point in your life. I start with Foundational life experiences, these are experiences that everyone should have. Second I move onto standard life experiences, these are common experiences that a lot of people have, but are not necessary for everyone. Third includes some unique experiences you might not have considered. Fourth are riskier options and how to assess/minimize risk. Finally I talk about travel and living abroad.

Foundational Experiences:

My opinion is that everyone should have these foundational experiences at some point in their lives and if you haven't already had any of the following experiences you should get on it as soon as possible. The following teach fundamental skills which might seem silly to people who are already past that point in their life, but people who haven't had these foundational experiences will benefit greatly by going through with them.

Earning your own Money and Paying for Rent and Groceries

This book is directed at people from all different age groups. If you have never supported yourself financially, this should be the first thing you do in your experience phase. By covering your own expenses you will learn very basic, but important skills like cleaning your place, buying food and other daily items, managing your own sleep schedule etc. It doesn't matter if you rent your own apartment or if you share a house with friends. What matters is that you cover your own expenses yourself.

Traveling or Living Abroad

I'm not saying that everyone needs to go on a 5 year long backpacking adventure around the world, but I would say that everyone should spend at least some time in a foreign country. Ideally you travel alone and the countries you visit are very different compared to wherever you are from. When you go abroad you are forced to interact with a brand new culture and in many cases a new language. This tests your ability to deal with loneliness, to meet new people and it shows you what it feels like to be an outsider (in case you have never felt that before). It also takes you away from your family and friends, which allows you to see who you really are independent from their influences. This separation can result in rapid personality transformation.

Start up Conversations with at least 100 Strangers

Some people naturally start up conversations with strangers so they likely already have had this experience dozens of times over. Other people have never even started a conversation with a stranger one time in their entire life. It doesn't really matter where you meet them, it could be on the street, at a bar, at school, or anywhere you want. So long as you are the one initiating the conversation. Also, it doesn't matter how long the conversation lasts, it counts if you just exchange a few words.

Before I started intentionally meeting lots of new people I was very limited in terms of the sorts of people I knew. I was only connected to a few different social groups as well as to my family. Even if you meet a lot of people through your social circles you will still be limited in terms of who you interact with. When you initiate conversations yourself you end up interacting with a much broader range of people. Another benefit is the increase in confidence that you get from approaching so many people. It can be a bit unnerving to start up a conversation with a stranger, but the act of overcoming that anxiety will make you mentally stronger.

Standard Experiences

All of the **standard experiences** in this section are widely known, in fact you probably know a lot of people who have done most of these things. There is no shame in pursuing standard experiences, they are standard because they are recognized as great experiences. Some people feel like they have to do something unique, but most of the best options have already been well-trodden. Sure, you can include some unique experiences as well, this is probably a good idea, but if you avoid standard experiences entirely you will miss out.

Long-term Budget Travel

This experience is becoming more and more popular every year. And with good reason. Long-term budget travel is a great way to get to know lots of different countries, experience a wide array of cultures, and consistently get out of your comfort zone on a daily basis. Most people call it backpacking because you typically travel from place to place with all of your stuff in one large backpack. I don't always use this term because backpacking can be confused with long hikes in the wilderness, which is a different experience that I will recommend later on.

Become a Sports/Surf/Ski Enthusiast

This applies to all kinds of different outdoor sports like skiing, hiking, climbing, diving and more. The idea is that you move to the best surfing destinations in the world and live there for months or even years. Depending on your sport you may need to move around the world to make sure that you are always in the perfect place to practice. To make this work you might need to be careful with money and take on a local job. Most people who live this lifestyle end up sharing a room with a few other people to make ends meet.

Living and Working Abroad

This experience is a bit tricky and might not be an option for everyone. I was lucky and the company that I had worked for in Canada has an office in Germany, they actually invited me to go work there. I spent more than two years working in Germany on and off. Many people find work teaching English all over the world. The highest paying countries are Japan, Korea, China, and to a lesser extent Chile and Vietnam. The problem is that most of these countries require that you are a native English speaker and have a University Degree.

There are lots of other options for teaching English around the world, but most of these jobs don't actually pay very well. In addition to teaching English there are also tons of other opportunities for lower-skilled workers in many different countries, but those jobs usually don't pay well either. If you want a higher paying job in a foreign country it is certainly a possibility, you just need the necessary experience. Many experienced workers will actually earn more money in a foreign country.

Join the Armed Forces

This is a great idea for certain people in certain countries, especially younger people who don't have much in terms of career prospects. In some countries you can join the armed forces for a couple of years and they will provide various kinds of technical training. In the process you will develop a lot of skills like willpower, physical fitness, leadership etc. One huge advantage of joining the armed forces at the beginning of your experience phase is that by the end of your contract you will actually have some money saved up, you can then go on to travel or do whatever else you wanted to do. An armed forces contract works well with a longer experience phase. For example, four years in the armed forces and then 2 years traveling, but you can plan it out however you want.

Dedicate Yourself to a Spiritual School or a Specific Skill

This may or may not involve traveling to a new place, after all it is often possible to find a good school in your home town. But, some people find that they learn more moving away. This is partially because they can make sure to choose the best school, but also because they won't be distracted by their family and friends. The diligence and humility that you develop by spending months or even years focusing on a single pursuit will serve you throughout the course of your entire life. Consider living in an ashram, joining a meditation retreat, learning a martial art, or practicing dance.

Live in the Wilderness

No electricity except flashlight batteries and cut out all connections with the outside world. You can do this on your own or with friends. Beginners will find a few days out in the wilderness to be an interesting experience, people who have camped before should consider spending a week or even longer completely disconnected from society. There is a special feeling you get when you are completely disconnected from the busyness of the modern world, you are able to be completely alone with your thoughts.

For most of us, in our regular lives, we are constantly bombarded by stimuli from electronic media, work, family, etc. Our brains never truly get a chance to relax. When you go out into the wilderness for days or even weeks at a time your brain gets a break from these stimuli. Note: going out into the wilderness is much easier for certain people in certain countries. I have been to a lot of countries where leaving the safety of civilization is actually fairly dangerous because you need to watch out for poisonous insects, snakes, thieves etc. However, where I am from, it is fairly safe to go into the woods. But, of course, you need to be careful everywhere.

Perform

Many people have a strong desire to do some kind of artistic performance. Some kids always wanted to be a rockstar or maybe a rapper. Being a performer never really appealed to me, but I know that it is a typical dream for a lot of young people. This includes any kind of live performance like comedy, dance, or whatever appeals to you. It is worth your while to try out some open mic nights, at least find some kind of way to perform. I suspect that this would be nerve wracking for a beginner.

Create Something with your Hands

This includes painting, woodworking, pottery, sculpting, sewing, crocheting, and a lot more. While this particular experience doesn't appeal to me at all, I know that it is something that a lot of people are drawn to. Many people feel that because they never work with their hands they are missing out on something fundamental to the human experience. So if you feel a strong desire to build something or if you find these kinds of projects appealing it is worth trying out. You can start by watching YouTube videos or even going to a class.

This particular experience works great for travelers, but you would be surprised how many avid travelers only speak 1 or 2 languages. If you go to a foreign country where many of the local people speak a different language, learning that language will open up all kinds of opportunities you might not expect.

Yes, you can still make local friends without learning the local language, but you will only be able to befriend locals who speak English. Generally speaking, this means more educated wealthier people or people who work in tourism. In some parts of the world, many countries in Latin America for example, it is common to find very well educated people who barely speak English. I am in Peru right now and I very rarely meet anyone who speaks English outside of tour operators.

If you don't plan on traveling, learning a language may still be an interesting experience. I have always found learning languages through pure study to be very difficult and boring, but some people do seem to be able to do it. You can take a language class, use an application like duolingo, consume media in the language (movies, television, books, etc.), or even make friends online and Skype them in their language.

There is some evidence which suggests that learning a language may make you smarter and this is consistent with my own experiences. For example, my competitive chess playing ability skyrocketed after learning Spanish.

A large part of our thinking involves words and sentences. When we learn a new language we learn to think using new words and new sentence structures. I believe that this increases our cognitive flexibility and as a result it improves our overall cognitive function.

Volunteer

A lot of people find that taking on some kind of meaningful volunteer work is a life-changing experience which benefits them for the rest of their lives. When I was in high school I volunteered in a senior center playing board games with the local residents. Most days I would play chess with a disabled man who was an immigrant from the Philippines. He was wheelchair bound and didn't have the motor control to speak, but he could still play great chess.

Volunteering is supposed to be about helping other people or working on some kind of project, but likely you will find that it benefits you just as much as the people you are trying to help. If you do decide to volunteer in a foreign country I suggest staying for at least a year if not longer. There has been a recent trend of people from wealthier countries paying a lot of money "help" people in poor countries. This is known as voluntourism and may cause more harm than good. If you do want to volunteer in a poor country it is best that you have some kind of useful skills or are willing to learn. Note: there are also probably lots of organizations in your hometown who need able bodies.

Do a Manual Labor Job

Not everyone has the physical health to do this, but if you are able to keep up I suggest taking on a manual labor job at some point in your life. You will develop a lot of mental grit and physical fitness as well.

Compete in a Sport or a Martial Art

There is something unique to be learnt by competing. You get to actually test your abilities under pressure. When you play for fun all the time it is possible to convince yourself that you are actually better than you really are, this is because it is easier rationalize your losses and take credit for your wins. For example, you can tell yourself that you weren't really trying when you lost, but you might not give your opponents the same credit when you win. However, in a tournament setting, no one is holding back.

The other advantage of competition is that it is stressful, any insecurities you have will be amplified in your mind. You will learn a lot about yourself by watching how you perform under the stress of competition. Another advantage of competing in a sport or a martial art is that you will need to achieve peak levels of physical fitness in preparation for the competition. If you have never had the experience of being extremely fit, you should try to get there at least once. Non-physical games like chess might give you some of the benefits of a sport, but they won't get you into awesome physical shape.

Sell Something on the Street

It doesn't matter if you are selling handicrafts or trying to get people to donate to a charity, this is a great opportunity to really put yourself on the line. The reality of trying to sell something on the street is that you will get rejected much more often than you succeed, people just don't want to be bothered, they have other things on their mind for the day. Getting to a point where rejection doesn't bother you at all is a very liberating feeling. It allows you to do all kinds of other things in your life.

When I was in University I volunteered for a couple of different psychology labs. One summer I had to approach people in the Student Union Building and ask them if to participate in a psychology survey. This was certainly easier than trying to sell something, but it was still a bit nerve wracking because many of the people I approached actually rejected me. After doing this I became much more confident approaching people, which is a skill that helped me meet people in other situations.

Unique Experiences

Live and Work in the Same Building

This is a really good idea if you want to go traveling. There are some jobs where you get your food and accommodation covered while you literally live at your place of work. Some possibilities are working on a cruise ship or commercial fishing. It might be uncomfortable for some people because you can't really get away from work, but that is the point, to be uncomfortable. My job right now actually covers food and accommodation. I don't work year round, only 3-6 months of the year. This is how I have been able to travel the world and actually save money at the same time.

Live in a Commune

I am going to use this term commune very loosely. I just mean any place where people get together and share all of their belongings. In most modern societies, particularly in the west, people have a strong attachment to ownership. Yes, this makes a lot of sense especially when it comes to big things like your house, your bank account etc. But, it is an interesting experience to live in a way where no one really owns anything. There are all kinds of communes all over the world, just research your area.

Go to Burning Man

Every year, starting in late August, 70 000+ people come together for a week in Black Rock Desert, Nevada. The event started at Baker Beach, California in 1986 with just a dozen people as a celebration of the summer solstice. Burning Man grew very quickly and by 1996 there were more than 8000 attendees.

Everyone who goes to Burning Man has their own interpretations of what the festival is about. People who haven't been there sometimes see it as a week-long music festival in the desert, but it is much more than that. I see Burning Man as a giant social experiment. Testing the limits of human societies. At Burning Man there is no money, you can't buy anything and you aren't even allowed to trade items. Meaning you can't say "I will give you this can of tuna for a cup of coffee". However, you are allowed to give things away, Burning Man calls itself a "Gift Economy".

Artists travel from all over the world to showcase their incredible creativity. Explore the desert at night and you might chance upon the mobile musical octopus which shoots fire out of its tentacles. Or enter the "Thunderdome" and battle it out Mad Max style.

If you do decide to go to make sure that you prepare properly. One of the principles at Burning Man is "Radical Self-Reliance", meaning that you should plan on contingencies and don't expect anyone else to take care of you. The climate is severe and you can't buy supplies anywhere. I can remember some days the sandstorms were so powerful that I couldn't even see my hand in front of my face. If you do your research and bring the stuff you need the harsh climate shouldn't bother you at all.

Burning Man is the ultimate playground for adults. Participate, experiment, and discover new things about yourself you didn't know existed.

Travel to Your Ethnic Homeland

This doesn't apply to people who already live in their ethnic homeland. But, if you are the descendant of foreigners, traveling to your ethnic homeland can be an interesting experience. One thing to keep in mind is that it will probably be underwhelming. Many people I have known who visited their ethnic homeland end up feeling disappointed, they often realize that they actually belong in the country in which they were born.

Go on a Pilgrimage

A pilgrimage is a journey to some place of spiritual significance, normally a very long walk. People have been going on spiritual pilgrimages for millennia. Your particular pilgrimage doesn't necessarily have to be spiritual, but you might find that a certain amount of spirituality makes your experience more interesting at least. In the modern day the most famous pilgrimages include the Camino de Santiago in southwestern Europe, the Kumano trail in Japan, and the Inca Trail in Peru. Personally, I have never been on a pilgrimage, but most people report that it is a life-changing experience. Naturally, the adventure itself is awesome, but also some people experience an altered state of consciousness once they reach the final point of their journey.

Have an Intense Spiritual Experience or Reach an Altered State of Consciousness

One thing I have discovered over the course of my life is that human beings are capable of a much broader range of conscious experiences than I had originally realized. In some cultures these "altered states of consciousness" are widely accepted as a part of ordinary life, but in other cultures, particularly in the west, altered states of consciousness are generally ignored or vilified.

What exactly do I mean by an altered state of consciousness? I am specifically referring to states of mind which are not experienced in ordinary waking life. These states can be induced through meditation, sensory deprivation, hypnosis, fasting, psychedelic drugs, and more. By my definition stimulant and opiate drugs don't induce a true altered state of consciousness, because they are simply concentrated versions of states of mind which occur in ordinary life.

Altered states of consciousness include, but are not limited to, hallucinations, synesthesia, a sensation of being transported into another universe, ego-death, dissociation with one's own body, losing one's sense of self, and feelings of unconditional love for everyone and everything. Between the ages of 18-22 I became fascinated by altered states of consciousness and experimented with a lot of different methods for inducing these states of mind. I grew up nonreligious and without strong spiritual inclinations so the idea of experiencing different kinds of spiritual experiences fascinated me. The very concept of experiencing "new forms" of consciousness was intriguing and I certainly wasn't disappointed with the results.

One of the first things I tried out was a sensory deprivation tank. This is a device which was invented by Dr. John Lilly in 1954. It is designed in such a way as to completely eliminate any kind of sensory input. When the brain is denied sensory input it starts to produce all kinds of hallucinations. A floatation tank is a soundproof, light proof, tank of water which is filled with hundreds of pounds of Epsom salts. The idea is that you float inside of the tank for an extended period of time and over the course of your "float" you will likely experience some kind of altered state of consciousness.

Some people hear about sensory deprivation tanks and they don't understand the appeal. They ask how is it different from lying down in the bathtub with the lights off?

1. The bathtub isn't totally soundproof
2. Unless the tub is huge you will still feel the sides of the tub.
3. You will sink to the bottom of a normal bath.
4. A sensory deprivation tank is heated to 34 degrees Celsius, close to the temperature of your skin. The bathtub will likely be too hot or too cold creating sensory input.

There needs to be no sensory input at all or else it won't work. In your bathtub, you might have a relaxing evening, but you likely won't have an altered state of consciousness.

Altered states of consciousness can make you very suggestible and transform your behavior over the long-term. The first time I used a sensory deprivation tank it was in a random apartment in North Vancouver, I found the "company" through a Google search. My first float was 90 minutes long and I really enjoyed the experience. It felt like I was floating in space without seeing any stars or planets. While there were visual hallucinations, the most interesting sensation was that I didn't even feel like I was lying down, I felt like I could be oriented vertically, horizontally, or upside down. At times it felt like I was rotating on the vertical axis and other times it felt like I was rotating on the horizontal axis.

A month later I went back to the same spot and I had another float. There were two brothers running the company, the second time I floated it was the other brother who was supervising. My float was supposed to be 90 minutes long, and unbeknownst to me at the time he decided to let me float a lot longer. While you are floating you have no idea how much time is passing and you have to wait for the supervisor to knock and let you out. I'm not sure how long I floated, but I am grateful that he decided to give me bonus time. During my experience, I went really deep into my insecurities and weaknesses.

I had always been an active kid, but for two years I had stopped exercising due to an ACL tear. Not a great excuse, I could still ride a bike and do other exercises, but I was a teenager and didn't have that discipline required to exercise without sports. As a result of my inactivity I became depressed and out of shape, during my time in the tank I resolved to commit myself to getting in shape. Since this experience I have been able to consistently follow an exercise routine for the past 8 years without skipping a single workout. My routines have changed quite a bit, but I have always followed through. I credit this resolve to the transformative power of altered states of consciousness.

Meditation, floatation tanks, fasting, etc. are all effective methods for reaching a spiritual experience, but they don't work for everyone and may require a lot of effort. Some people go on 10-day meditation retreats and don't even have a spiritual experience in the process.

Psychedelics are a complicated subject. They certainly produce altered states of consciousness, but they come with more potential risks. Psychedelics have the power to drastically transform people's personalities in one afternoon, but the transformations aren't necessarily positive.

My warning about the potential dangers of psychedelics applies to all altered states of consciousness. In these states you have the power to dramatically improve your behavior and personality forever, you become extremely malleable. An analogy is when a blacksmith heats up metal, it can then be formed into a new shape. But, in this state, you are also vulnerable. Just as you can be transformed into something positive, you can also be transformed into something negative.

Some spiritual people make the mistake of believing that any altered state of consciousness is a good thing, actually altered states of consciousness are neutral. They are a powerful tool and any powerful tool can be used irresponsibly. It doesn't matter if you are doing something which seems harmless like meditation, you can still potentially cause damage.

So venture into the world of altered states of consciousness with caution and be careful who you surround yourself with during these states of mind.

Higher-Risk Experiences

With any experience, or really anything we do in life, it is important to do a risk-benefit analysis. Most people have at least a couple of higher-risk experiences that they really want to have at some point in their lives. Naturally, the question of higher-risk experiences, is a bit contentious. For some people the idea of taking a risk just for the purpose of having an experience is immature and self-destructive. Other people risk their lives/financial stability on a nearly daily basis.

The first thing I want to point out is that life is never without danger. Automobile accidents kill a lot of people, a financial crisis could leave you bankrupt, and you or someone you love could (and probably will someday) discover that they have an incurable life-threatening disease. Because of these dangers and many more dangers we have to conclude that true safety is an illusion. Any day a meteor or a superbug could kill all advanced life on planet earth, ask an expert, these are both very realistic events. So it is impossible to live risk-free.

By saying this I am certainly not giving you permission to take wild irresponsible risks. Don't forget that if you get injured, die, or lose all your savings you not only damage yourself, but you also cause immense suffering to the people around you. Personally, I am not terribly afraid to die, but I recognize the investment that other people put into me at a young age and I also understand how much negativity my death would cause to the people close me. This is why I always take a rational calculated cold-blooded approach to risk and I suggest you do the same.

One Small Adjustment

Many experiences can be transformed from very high risk to low risk with one small concession. The most obvious example is casual sex. Casual sex is never risk free, there is always the possibility of psychological damage, sexually transmitted diseases, and/or unwanted pregnancy. Unprotected casual sex is very risky, in fact there are very few activities which are as risky as unprotected casual sex, at least when it comes to things that a lot of people engage in. Casual sex with protection is still potentially dangerous, but the risk factor is much much lower. The main risks of casual sex with protection are emotional damage and some of the less severe sexually transmitted infections.

Many extreme sports have a dangerous variation and a more safe variation. Paragliding is a perfect example. I have recently started researching paragliding and I have discovered that it is actually very safe. Despite the fact that you are literally flying through the air at the mercy of sometimes unpredictable air currents very few people actually die or experience serious injury paragliding.

But, there is a similar sport called speed flying. Unlike Paragliders who fly hundreds of feet above the ground for long periods of time, speed flyers get as close to the ground as possible which allows them to fly much faster. Watching speed flyers launch themselves down a mountain through a gopro reminds me of a skier barrelling down a slope. Almost all paragliding accidents happen when the pilot is close to the ground, speed flyers literally put themselves into the most dangerous situation possible. For most people paragliding alone is a massive rush and there is no reason to take it to the next level, but in order to get that extra rush speed flyers increase the risk factor dramatically.

There are plenty of other examples of extreme sports which can be done safely or unsafely. Skydiving and base jumping is a another example. Skydiving is pretty safe, many people have hundreds or even thousands of jumps under their belt without any injuries at all. Base jumping, on the other hand, is extremely dangerous. Base jumping is where you climb up a mountain and jump off the side with a parachute. You only have a few seconds to pull your chute and in many cases base jumpers successfully pull their chute but end up colliding into the mountain on release. In some cases skydiving there are equipment failures, but there are also plenty of alternative options in this case (like a reserve parachute).

In traveling many of the countries I wanted to visit were dangerous. It's not that I had some particular attraction to dangerous countries, in fact a large number of the countries I have visited have also been totally safe, rather, I simply didn't allow the fear of getting robbed/kidnapped stop me from going places I wanted to go. But does that mean that when I went to dangerous countries I was reckless and I didn't pay attention to my surroundings? Not at all. There are very few countries which are actually too dangerous to visit, but on the other hand many countries have the potential to be dangerous if you aren't careful.

When I was in Honduras in 2014 it was considered to be the most dangerous country in the world, at least excluding pure war zones. When I was there I didn't go out at night, I stayed on busy roads, and I was always cautious with who I talked to. Compare that to Nicaragua, a country bordering Honduras, which is considered by many to be the safest country in Central America. A lot of people who visit Nicaragua get mugged or worse. What do you think is more dangerous? Traveling through Honduras cautiously or traveling through Nicaragua recklessly. Just like extreme sports, cautious travel in dangerous countries is hundreds of times safer than reckless travel in those same countries.

When deciding whether or not to take on a dangerous experience the first thing to consider is whether or not there is a way to reduce the risk without losing the integrity of the experience itself. I believe that in many cases it is possible to dramatically reduce the risk while not affecting the experience very much. Ultimately, if a particular experience is just straight up physically/financially dangerous and there is nothing you can do about that danger I don't recommend following through with it. Being in an experience phase doesn't protect you in any special way, you can still take on physical, financial, and emotional damage. That being said, doing nothing is the greatest risk. If you aren't able to tolerate any amount of danger you won't experience anything at all, and that is much worse than dying doing something you love.

On Travel

When we are talking about the experience phase and what you should do it is impossible not to talk about travel. For some people most of the experiences that they want to have are travel experiences, but other people have no interest in traveling at all. Of course, traveling was a huge part of my own experience phase, but I understand that for other people this isn't necessarily the case. That's why I am making a conscious effort to talk about other options in this book. That being said, this section will be all about travel and living abroad.

There are a lot of different ways you can work travel into your life. Personally, I chose to take on a long-term travel lifestyle as well as work abroad. By my definition, the long-term travel lifestyle is where you completely move out of your apartment, house etc. If you are renting you end your lease and if you own then you find tenants to rent out your home. You get rid of everything that you can't carry in a medium sized backpack (around 60 liters) or if necessary you get a storage locker. For the past four years everything I own fits into a 35-liter and a 20-liter backpack. This long-term travel lifestyle has a lot of advantages and disadvantages. Here are the advantages:

- Easy mobility in terms of moving from place to place.

- Lower cost of living because you don't have to pay monthly rent. At least compared to traveling and keeping your apartment/house at the same time.

- An enormous sense of freedom, no attachment to material objects. By getting rid of your stability you commit 100% to the travel lifestyle.

Here are the disadvantages:

- Certain experiences involve equipment, which is difficult to carry around with you everywhere. E.g. a surfboard, a winter jacket, skis, etc.

- No backup option in case you get tired of traveling. You have to completely rebuild your life when you are done.

- Some people are unable to live without any stability.

- Difficult or impossible to find work.

I was very fortunate in that I still hadn't accumulated many material objects when I started the long-term travel lifestyle, It was fairly easy to get rid of everything I owned. Over time most people accumulate more and more material objects, naturally these objects tie you down to living in one place. If you are in this position where you already have a lot of belongings consider getting a storage locker or perhaps finding someone who doesn't mind living with your stuff.

For most people, long-term travel is also budget travel. Usually people don't have the money to travel around the world living luxuriously. The reality of long-term travel is that it is normally all about saving money. A lot of people do manage to travel around the world for months or even years, but nearly all of them are paying close attention to every penny they spend. Most people would be shocked if they saw some of the places I slept in or some of the food I ate, and I am not even the most extreme.

This might sound like a miserable life, but in reality you get used to it over time. Actually taking an extreme approach to budget travel usually results in more interesting travel experiences. Instead of taking a luxury bus choose the cheapest local bus. This will give you a better understanding of how local people actually live, in some countries the person next to you might have a chicken on their lap. Another example is with food. Instead of going out to nice restaurants go to local markets or eat street food. A lot of people say that it is worth your while to spend your money on great travel experiences and I believe that this is true, but often the best travel experiences can only be had by being cheap.

Generally speaking, when it comes to long-term travel (2 months or more), it is better to choose one part of the world at a time and visit a number of different countries in that area. After spending a few months (or years) in this area then you can then consider going to a new part of the world. The most obvious reason why this is a good idea is that the countries are in close proximity, so traveling between countries is faster and cheaper. Also, it is a good idea because most countries usually share cultural similarities with their neighbors, so as you spend more and more time in a particular area you get more and more comfortable with the culture.

Some regions even share the same language, i.e. Spanish in Latin America, Swahili in East Africa, and Bahasa in Malaysia/Indonesia. So if you are going to commit to long-term travel I suggest committing yourself to certain long-term travel routes. The awesome thing about this form of travel is that you don't have to plan out your entire journey exactly, the countries are all so close together that you can usually spontaneously go to any of the countries in the region. Here are some of the most common long-term travel routes:

Southeast Asia:

Overall Southeast Asia is the best long-term travel route for most people. It is cheap, safe, and filled with endless beautiful sights and attractions. You could go to Southeast Asia for a few weeks or travel there for years on end. By my own definition Southeast Asia includes Thailand, Cambodia, Vietnam, Laos, The Philippines, Malaysia, Indonesia, and possibly Singapore/Myanmar. That's a lot of different countries and there are a ton of different things that you can do. As you might expect there are a lot of beaches, but there are also mountains, jungles, and vibrant cities. If you are planning a long-term travel route through Southeast Asia I suggest starting in Bangkok or Kuala Lumpur. Both of these cities are well developed with a strong tourist infrastructure. Also, both Thailand and Malaysia offer visas on arrival to people from most countries. Once you are comfortable in either city you can move on to other places.

Latin America:

Arguably this could be split up into Central America and South America. But some people actually go through Central America and South America in one long trip. Not many people speak English in this part of the world, but Spanish is widely spoken. After a few months of travel you should have strong enough Spanish to at least get by. In my opinion the best part about visiting Latin America are the people that you meet. Locals can be unbelievably friendly and interesting. In addition to the people there are also tons of beautiful attractions.

Latin America is one of the most dangerous regions in the world, but that shouldn't stop you from coming here. I am in Peru right now and after meeting a lot of other travelers who have been through Latin America most of them insist that it isn't very dangerous after all.

Europe:

You could split Europe up into many different categories. Naturally Portugal is very different culturally from Russia. But for simplicity I am going to talk about Europe as a whole. Most of Europe is fairly expensive compared to the rest of the world, but that is made up for in terms of organization and safety. Most European countries are relatively safe and getting around is fairly easy. In my experience, the best part about traveling in Europe is the food and the architecture.

European cities and towns are the most beautiful in the world, people seem to place a special importance on aesthetics. Also, the food culture is amazing, nearly every single region within every country has a unique culinary flavor. The only thing I missed in European food was the spiciness you find in Asian cuisine. Also, if you like wine or beer, it is usually ridiculously cheap in Europe.

East Africa

Probably the most difficult travel route on this list. While East African countries are surprisingly safe, the tourist infrastructure is sometimes terrible. If you go on an organized tour you will get around fine, but I am assuming that you want to travel independently. You probably won't see a lot of other travelers, so you will end up needing to rely on your street smarts to get around. By my definition, the East African travel route includes Ethiopia, Kenya, Uganda, Rwanda, Burundi, Tanzania, and Malawi. I don't recommend traveling through East Africa as a first time traveler, unless you plan on going with a tour group.

***

These are just some of the long-term travel routes. There are plenty of other options like the Middle East, India and the countries surrounding India, Southern African countries like Zambia and Botswana, East Asia, as well as North America. For more information on long-term travel including a whole series on travel for beginners check out my blog worldcitizenevan.com.

It is perfectly reasonable to fit travel into your life while also living a more normal lifestyle. This is what almost everyone on the planet actually does. If you are a hardcore traveler who lives the long-term travel lifestyle it is easy to forget that this is a pretty atypical way of living. The challenge with living a more normal lifestyle is that your costs will be higher and as a result you will probably have to take on an ordinary job.

When you live the long-term travel lifestyle your costs are so low that there are lots of atypical jobs which can support you financially and your income will likely be low enough to keep you in a low tax bracket. But if you are trying to travel, pay rent, electricity etc. Your costs will be much higher and as a result you will need to earn more money and pay more taxes.

Most people working ordinary jobs with 40-hour workweeks or more often feel frustrated with their lives and try to compensate for their existential angst by buying things. They feel like they have to justify their hard work or at least reward themselves for it. So, chances are you won't have a lot of extra money for travel. I would say that if you have a lot of different travel dreams and that they are highly important to you, living the long-term travel lifestyle is a necessity. Trying to fit travel into a normal life only works for people who don't see travel as one of the main priorities in their life.

Another excellent option is to actually work abroad. This is a better option than long-term travel for a lot of people. Especially people who are able to find reasonable jobs abroad which are coherent with their career. Working abroad means that you won't have to spend your money in order to see the world and if you are careful you might actually save money in the foreign country.

When you work abroad and spend more time in a single place you will get to know that culture much better, make close friends, and possibly learn the local language. A lot of long-term travelers barely develop any local friendships or language skills at all. The main disadvantage of working abroad is that you might not be able to choose where you go, you certainly won't have as much freedom as in long-term travel. But, I think that the advantages of working abroad certainly compensate for the disadvantages. One option is to work abroad, save money, and then travel after.

Another possibility is to find a job/business where you can work online and earn money while you are traveling. This might sound awesome, but it is actually pretty hard to concentrate on work while you are moving quickly from place to place. I find that it is a lot easier to work if I stay in each place for at least a month. Working online and traveling is great, but it isn't all fun and games. It can be a lot harder to buckle down and get to work when you don't have a routine and you are on your own (without coworkers).

Whether you are working abroad or traveling short/long-term, it is always best to approach the situation actively rather than passively. Meaning that you should try to engage with the environment in front of you rather than simply taking it in. If you see some snacks for sale on the side of the road walk over and try one. When you are in a taxi start up a conversation with the driver. When you are on a tour ask the guide lots of questions. Actively engaging while you are traveling is beneficial for a few different reasons:

1. It will result in all kinds of interesting opportunities. Just by being friendly to people you have no idea what might happen. They might invite you over for dinner or show you some awesome places that most tourists don't know anything about.

2. By actively engaging with the environment in front of you will be more likely to remember that moment. If you don't actively engage the whole trip will probably be a blur in your mind.

Also, when you are traveling, break patterns. If you have been to a lot of big cities, go to a small town. If you have spent a lot of time in nature, go to a big city. This will make your trip more memorable and squeeze as much impact as possible out of your travels. Another way to make your trip more memorable is to write a lot. If you don't write at all during your travels you will probably remember what you did, but it might be hard to remember exactly what you were feeling on a day to day basis. In the future you will appreciate the fact that you can look back and see how your thoughts and ideas progressed over time.

Travel Traps

Some people, when they go abroad, fall into the trap of drinking/partying too much. In fact, I know travelers who partied every single night for months and months straight. There is something about getting out of your home country that makes certain people want to get crazy. There's nothing wrong with partying occasionally, but if it becomes a central part of your travels something is seriously wrong.

Another common trap is that travelers (as well as people working abroad) end up spending all of their time with other foreigners from similar countries. I know of people who have been all over Latin America but barely speak any Spanish at all because they only befriended fellow foreigners. I think hostels are a great option for a lot of people but it is very easy to fall into the trap of only meeting other travelers when you are staying at a hostel. The same thing goes for touristic cafes and bars. On my blog, I talk a lot about meeting locals in foreign countries. Check out https://worldcitizenevan.com/the-beginning-travelers-handbook/

Going abroad at least once should be a part of everyone's experience phase, but whether your experience phase is based around travel or not depends entirely on you. Perhaps you just aren't comfortable quitting your job and would prefer to work your experience phase around a normal workweek. That is a reasonable approach for a lot of people.

Final Thoughts on What to Do

It's good to choose experiences that will benefit you over the long run, but that isn't the main goal, it's all about choosing the things that you really want to do. Why choose experiences which may or may not benefit you? Why not just choose things which you will definitely be of benefit over the long-run? Two reasons:

1. Experiences are valuable in and of themselves. They don't have to benefit you in any way to be worth your time. Note: if an experience is particularly risky or expensive, it's probably not worth it

unless it actually benefits you over the long run. But, if it isn't very risky or expensive it is probably worth your time.

2. You don't necessarily know if an experience will benefit you over the long-run. It's hard to know exactly how something will affect you and how it will inform you. An experience might seem inconsequential at first, but then over time you realize how much it actually benefited you. I can remember a couple of times, first in Guatemala and then in Nicaragua, fellow travelers asked me to climb a volcano with them. I didn't really want to go either time, but I let them convince me. I ended up really enjoying myself and these experiences contributed to me developing a passion for climbing mountains.

To truly go deep into the experience phase you must immerse yourself into whatever you are doing, forget the past and the future, and chase adventure like your life depends on it.

9
Planning and Choosing the Optimal Length

The length of an experience phase will vary quite a bit depending on your particular situation. Some people are able to fit an experience phase into a summer break in between University semesters and other people will spend an entire decade in their experience phase. My own experience phase lasted for 5 years, which might seem like a long time to some people, but in the context of your entire life it isn't actually that long. 5 years was the perfect amount of time for me to live through almost all of my own particular dreams, this chapter is about figuring out how long your own experience phase should be.

It is very important that you actually set a time limit for your experience phase. As I mentioned in a previous chapter you don't want to get stuck in the experience phase for the rest of your life. While it may be possible to self-regulate or to set another limit (other than time), I think a time limit is a simple straightforward approach.

The shortest period of time I am willing to accept as an "experience phase" is two months. Yes you could have a lot of interesting life changing experiences in one week, but this isn't really a phase, instead it is just an exciting week. The experience phase needs to be long enough to make it memorable, it needs to be an actual phase of your life. I am going to give you a couple of different examples of different lengths of experience phases so you can understand your options better.

2-3 months: Maybe in between classes at University during a summer break or in between two different jobs. A 2-3 month experience phase is perfect for someone who values experiences, but sees other values (career, family, religion etc.) as more important. You certainly won't be able to squeeze much into a 2-3 month period, but the fact that you are rushed might encourage you to pursue experiences with even more passion, there is no doubt that even a shorter experience phase will still have lasting impact on your life.

6 months to 2 years: Popular in some cultures when students take on gap years in between high school and University or in the Amish tradition teenagers will have a 2 year Rumspringa. This length of experience phase is great for people who want to have a substantial number of different experiences in their life and also people who see experiences as important. But, it is still probably not long enough to be able to live out all of your dreams. A year long experience phase is long enough to save and travel to South America for example or it is long enough to train and the compete in a sport, but it will go by much faster than you expect.

3-5 years: This is the length of my own experience phase. I was able to save money, travel the world, meet hundreds of people, and live out almost all of my dreams. Personally I have always placed more importance on my experiences than on other values like career, family etc. Now that I have finished my experience phase my value hierarchy is changing. A 3-5 year experience phase should be more than enough time for most people especially if you have already had a decent number of experiences before beginning. I actually finished my bucket-list right when the experience phase was over, so anything less than 5 years wouldn't have been long enough. And anything more than 5 years would have been excessive.

5-10 years+: Extreme experience phase. This is for people who are ready to dedicate an enormous part of their life to experiences. Just to put this in context, if you are 25 years old and you have a 10 year experience phase you won't be done until you are 35 years old. Probably a very long experience phase is a good idea for people just starting adulthood (around 18-21) or for people who have already retired, have no financial obligations and are also in good health. There is no doubt that an extremely long experience phase will require sacrifices in other aspect of your life, but it may be worth it for certain people.

Your Mindset Improves over the Course of your Experience Phase

Consider the importance of being in an "experience mindset". Over time, as your experience phase progresses, your mindset will improve overall. You will more aggressively pursue new experiences and will have the correct mentality. If your experience phase is very short, i.e. a few months, you won't have enough time to completely settle into the best mindset. However, if your experience phase is a few years, you will have enough time to develop the right mentality. I think that my own particular mindset continued to improve throughout the course of my experience phase so I think that the longer your experience phase the better your mindset, at least your mindset applied to pursuing new experiences.

What do I mean by having the right mindset? That will be covered in the next chapter. But, in brief, the correct mindset is making sure to take opportunities to have new experiences when they come up, to pursue new experiences intentionally, and also to fully take advantage of the experiences that you are having.

Perhaps you are different and you are able to take on the right mentality immediately, in which case this isn't much of a consideration. Perhaps just knowing that your experience phase is short will be enough to motivate you to get into a good mentality right away. But, I suspect that there is a certain level most people can't reach without taking a longer experience phase.

Another benefit of a longer experience phase is that you can make drastic life changes which may make the pursuit of experiences much easier. One of these life changes is to move out of your house/apartment. During a shorter experience phase this would be an irrational decision, but if your experience phase is a few years or more and you are planning on traveling the world then ending your lease or renting out your house would be a very smart choice. This will dramatically reduce your costs and may even provide an income stream. I don't mean to imply that you need to travel during your experience phase, this is only an example.

How much Planning is Optimal?

When it came to my own experience phase I did have a list of certain experiences that I wanted to have, but I didn't have a particular order I wanted to do them in. I just went through the experiences in the order that felt right. When I originally conceived of this chapter I was going to suggest that you do the same as me, don't follow any particular order, just have your experiences whenever the time feels right. But, then I reminded myself that people have very different personalities. Some people might appreciate a bit more organization in their experience phase, they might do better if they have it all planned out. While I am capable of being organized I certainly prefer to fly by the seat of my pants whenever possible, but I know that many people are different from me.

One thing to keep in mind is that certain experiences may require planning to make them work. Particularly big treks in the wilderness or going to festivals like Burning Man. Note: long-term travel doesn't usually require much pre-planning. At this point in my travels I can get packed in one day and since I already have all my immunizations, the only pre-planning required for travel is the visa requirements for the country that I am going to visit. Otherwise I can travel on a day's notice. But, even if you aren't an experienced traveler, it still doesn't require much pre-planning, just a few weeks ahead of time.

Here is a **heuristic for figuring out how long your experience phase should be**. Create a list of all the experiences that you want to have and estimate how long it will take you to have those experiences and also how long it will take to save money and or prepare if that is necessary. Take the total and multiply it by three. There are a couple of different reasons why you want to have extra time.

1. New opportunities will come up, especially if you are in the experience mindset. People will see that mindset in you and offer to take you places, invite you to events, or all kinds of other things.

2. You will likely discover new experiences that you want to have during your experience phase. If you are meeting a lot of new people someone might tell you about an experience which strikes your interest.

3. You will get off track at least some of the time, nobody is perfect, you will probably spend some time just being lazy and not pursuing experiences properly. Also, you will need to dedicate some time to maintenance and doing logistical things (e.g. medical, legal, taxes).

4. At the beginning of your experience phase you will need to adapt to the new mindset. Give yourself extra time to warm-up and get into the right mode of thought.

A very important consideration when it comes to deciding how long your experience phase should be is how far along are you in your own experience journey. As I have mentioned before if you are very young and haven't had a lot of experiences naturally it makes more sense to plan out a longer experience phase. But, if you are a bit older and have already completed most of your bucket list you won't need to have a really long experience phase.

To illustrate this previous point here are some examples. if you are 19 years old and you have never left your parent's house, but you plan on learning new languages and traveling the world you will need a much longer experience phase. If you are in your 30s and have already lived through many of your goals, you might be smart to have a shorter experience phase.

Why is it Important to have a Time Limit?

Overall choosing the length of your experience phase is important because of two main reasons:

1. It prevents of you from staying in the experience phase for too long.

2. It gives you a time constraint. Parkinson's Law states "work expands so as to fill the time available for its completion." Ever notice how when you have a task with a deadline you finish it more quickly? The same thing applies to experiences. When you set yourself a deadline you will pursue those experiences more aggressively and will get them done within the time constraint.

But, don't make the time constraint too short. You don't want to be in a rush. Even if you could "finish" your experiences within a short period of time that doesn't necessarily mean that you should. You don't want to just have you experiences and get them over with, you want to give yourself enough to time enjoy and savor them.

10
Mindset and Action

As you might expect having the right mindset is very important during an experience phase. Not just to make sure that you actually follow through, but also to make sure that you get the most from your experiences.

There are a lot of different mindsets which are available to us in life. These different mindsets are important for different goals. The optimal mindset for concentration while writing is much different from the optimal mindset for lifting a really heavy weight. A mistake that a lot of people make is that they get stuck in one mode and use that mindset in the wrong situation. An example would be a scientist who spends all day analyzing physics equations, it would be a mistake for him to apply the same mindset which he uses at his work when he goes to party. At his job it is important for him to be very precise, analytical, and careful with his language, but at a party it is much more important to be enthusiastic and gregarious. Precise language and contemplative thought is no longer an asset, but instead a hindrance.

I think that this is a big part of maturation, learning how to change your mindset depending on the situation that you are in. Hopefully, as we get older, we learn to be comfortable in more and more situations. It can be challenging to transition from one mindset to another even if you know that it is a good idea. I can remember when I was taking a lot of math classes in University it was really hard for me to transition to a more social mindset. What I have learned as I have matured is that it is important to take some time to move from one state of mind to another, warming up is essential. Just as important is the art of understanding which mindset to use and also constantly developing/improving the mindsets in your arsenal.

Maintenance

It is critical to try your best to maintain every aspect of your life as much as possible during the experience phase. The experience phase is unsuccessful if you ruin other parts of your life. No matter how many amazing experiences you have, life goes on when the Experience Phase is over. It is possible that in certain cases you won't be able to completely maintain certain aspects of your life, in this case you want to maintain as much as possible, make sure that you don't completely let go and lose all the progress that you already made.

Fitness and health

For some people their experience phase will actually improve their health and fitness. These are people who are normally inactive, but who start experimenting with being more active during their experience phase. For example: someone who didn't play sports as a kid decides to try out tennis as an adult.

However, people who are already at an elite level of physical fitness might have to deal with some degree of loss throughout their experience phase, even if their experience phase involves a lot of physical activity. This is because their physical activity is less organized and less consistent. So here are my recommendations for maintaining general fitness and health throughout the experience phase. Note: these are meant to maintain fitness in someone who is already extremely fit, not for someone who is already out of shape.

1. Exercise every single day. Even if it is a light day, just make sure to always do something. Also most of your workouts should resemble what you used to do when you were originally developing your high level of fitness.
2. Eat healthy foods 80 percent of the time or more.
3. Limit your alcohol consumption and other unhealthy habits.

Finances

Before going into maintaining your finances during an experience phase I want to be clear about something. Never rely on someone else to pay for your experience phase. This means no support from parents, partner/spouse or anyone else. Unless of course you are actually working for this money somehow. You won't get nearly the same benefit from your experience phase if someone else is paying for it, it won't feel as real. I have noticed that the least happy travelers I met were people who had support from their parents or were using inheritance money.

You should either net zero or actually save money throughout the course of your experience phase. If you end with less money than you started with than you made a mistake. Remember, part of the experience phase is saving money for your experiences if it is necessary. I was lucky enough to find a job which worked well with my experience phase goals, this job actually allowed me to save a lot of money while traveling the world. If you are worried about spending too much money here is what you need to do.

1. Practice extreme frugality. Yes, you can spend on experiences, but otherwise avoid spending your money. When I was saving money to travel I went for months on end without ever going out to a restaurant for food or buying something that I didn't absolutely need. Whenever I was tempted to go out for a meal I would remind myself what 20 dollars could buy me in Ethiopia (or whichever other country I wanted to go to).

2. If you do decide to quit your job or go on a sabbatical don't be afraid to take on part-time work. The part-time work may be an interesting experience in itself. Many people find that the random jobs they take on to pay for their travels (or whatever else) turn out to be very enlightening. Even if you aren't able to handle it right now, during your experience phase you will have the right mentality to do something wild like work on a cruise ship or some kind of manual labor work. Usually the process of saving and earning money results in all kinds of interesting experiences.

Career

This is pretty similar to your finances, but is still a bit different so I decided to make it a separate section. By career I am not necessarily referring to some straightforward career like a doctor or a teacher. By career I am referring to your overall professional progress including but not limited to skill acquisition, reputation, and networking. Maybe you are an entrepreneur, a firefighter, an athlete, or a writer, by my definition these are all included in the term "career". Of course, many people don't have any career direction yet, so these individuals don't have to worry about maintaining their career. But, people who have built up some kind of work experience will need to make sure to manage their situation during their experience phase.

During my experience phase I quit my job a total of 4 times (the same job). As a world traveler I needed to quit my job in order to follow through with my goals. The important thing is that every time I quit my job I made sure to do it under optimal conditions.

1. I quit when it was convenient for the company, not for myself. Either there weren't very many customers at the time and it benefited the company to not have to pay me or I quit when I had fully trained a replacement.

2. I always maintained strong relationships with my coworkers and I always made sure to say goodbye in a friendly way (I didn't flip anyone off).

3. I tied up all my loose ends and left everything in the best condition possible.

4. I gave months of notice ahead of time.

If you need to quit your job to make your experience phase happen, I suggest doing it in the most respectable way possible and continue to work hard until the very last day. Actually, I suggest working even harder on your last day to leave a good impression.

On the other hand, maybe you are able to keep your job during your experience phase or maybe you are able to at least maintain part-time work. After a few years of quitting my job and traveling I was able to negotiate a deal with my company where I would work part-time for 3-6 months every year and travel for the rest of the time.

Of course if you are running your own business this presents a whole new host of problems. Possibly you can find someone to help run it while you are focusing on other things. Or perhaps you can actually maintain it reasonably well while pursuing experiences. Either way, it would be a shame if you had to completely abandon your business in order to pursue experiences.

Family and Friendships

When you are living the life of your dreams it is very easy to forget to pay attention to your family and friends. They might even be jealous of you which also won't help very much. However, there is no reason why you can't maintain connections, at least to the people that you truly care about.

Most connections can maintained with a small message every few months and for closer relationships you can send a message every couple of weeks. Also, if you are actually in the same city, you should make sure to see them every occasionally as well. But, with technology it is much easier to maintain connections with people than it used to be, don't underestimate the value of a video call.

If you must cut out connections to other people for an extended period of time (a meditation retreat for example), make sure to communicate that to the people you care about. Don't surprise them by cutting off communication randomly no matter how much fun you are having.

Mental Cheat Codes (Mantras)

Many different religions understand the power of reciting certain phrases. In Christianity there is prayer/litany, in witchcraft there are incantations, and in Hinduism and Buddhism there are mantras. These phrases are often recited ritualistically for years and are usually believed to have magical or divine power. I won't claim that by using these phrases you will be able to enact change in the external world, but I will testify to their incredible power in terms of reprogramming your own mind. Choose a couple of the following phrases, commit them to memory, and recite them in your day to day. You can recite them in your mind or out loud depending on what feels right. Some of the phrases might work for you, others might not, the best phrase is the one which provokes the strongest emotional reaction.

"Seek out challenges rather than avoiding them" - Josh Waitzkin, Tai Chi Push Hands World Champion, Brazilian Jiu Jitsu black belt, and chess prodigy (subject of the film Searching for Bobby Fischer). In 2008, after winning the Tai Chi Push Hands World Championship, Josh Waitzkin published his ingenious book "The Art of Learning". In this book Josh explains how he went from a complete beginner to a high level competitor and eventually a world champion in Tai Chi. He uses analogies from chess to describe important concepts in the art of learning (and eventually mastering) a new skill. Currently, Waitzkin doesn't do much in terms of self-promotion (not much social media or more traditional media), but he is sought after by elite athletes, businesspeople, and others trying to optimize their performance.

This particular mantra is useful to keep in mind throughout the day. It is particularly useful during your experience phase or when you are learning a skill. In the same way that I suggest erring on the side of boldness, I also suggest erring on the side of challenge. If you are climbing a mountain choose the more difficult path. Not sure what to do on any given day? Try something new and challenging. The reality is that the deepest and most meaningful forms of happiness comes from the struggle, comfort comes naturally. At the end of the day, when you have put in your work, you will get your comfort. Whether or not you worked hard. But, that satisfied feeling will only occur if you put in the extra effort to get out of your comfort zone.

"The only way to make sense out of change is to plunge into it, move with it, and join the dance." - Alan Watts. Alan Watts was one of the first people to accurately portray eastern philosophy in western countries. He was a cultural icon in the 1960s and still is in certain circles. When we are trying something new it is vital to not hold on to our previous of conceptions of who we are, instead we should embrace the new environment we find ourselves in. A simpler quote would be **"go with the flow"**. Arguably the simpler phrases are better because they are easier to remember, but the longer phrases may also be more effective because they contain richer information and are more unique. Choose whichever mantra feels right.

"In the province of the mind what one believes to be is true or becomes true within certain limits to be found experientially and experimentally. These limits are further beliefs to be transcended. In the mind, there are no limits." - John Lilly. I know that is a really long mantra, but I love it. If you prefer a shorter mantra you can go with **"In the province of the mind what one believes to be true is true or becomes true."** In this statement Lilly is speaking to the incredible power of the human mind. The quote might seem a bit odd, I will admit that he uses fairly disorienting language.

What does Lilly mean by the Province of the Mind? By this Lilly is differentiating between your mind/conscious experiences and the physical world around you. He isn't saying that you can use your mind to control physical reality, instead he is saying that through belief you can control your own mental reality and that there are no limits to your conscious experience.

This mantra may be complicated, but it is unbelievably powerful once you have mulled it over for a while. It may confuse some people at first (myself included), so take a few minutes, write it down, and make sure that you understand all the subtleties. It is one of the most powerful observations about the human mind (and possibly beings in general) that I have ever heard. There is actually a much longer variation of this quote, which is even deeper and more profound. I thought about including it, but I decided that it would distract too much from the rest of the chapter.

While this mantra applies specifically to the province of the mind, it can be used to enhance your abilities in the physical realm as well. To illustrate with an example you can't will yourself into being a better runner, but you can convince yourself that you enjoy running, and as a result your running will improve.

"When you think you're done, you're only at 40% of your body's capability." - David Goggins. If you haven't heard David Goggins' story look him up, his life is inspiring and incredible. To give a very brief synopsis David Goggins was an obese man who dropped more than

100 pounds in 2 months to become a navy seal. He also performed many extraordinary physical feats like running 100 miles in 19 hours without training and also breaking the world record for most pull-ups done in 24 hours.

What does this quote mean exactly? Goggins uses the analogy of a governor in a car. The car may be capable of going up to 200 miles per hour, but the governor actually limits the speed to 90 miles per hour. The human mind has a similar "governor" which limits our output, but it is possible to tap into this additional 60% even when we think we are completely done. How else could Goggins, a 240lb powerlifter run 100 miles without even training? The answer is that he was able to turn off the governor in his brain. Note: before you go out and run 100 miles without training it is important to note that Goggins seriously damaged his body and had to go to the hospital after the race, so there may be some value in the governor, but the point is that we can go so much further than we believe.

"Fear is the mind killer" - Bene Gesserit litany against fear. The Bene Gesserit are a sisterhood from the science fiction series Dune. They have an ancient secret tradition of intense physical and mental exercises which gives their members superhuman abilities. The Bene Gesserit use their litany against fear to remain emotionally stable during moments of intense danger. One thing which stops many people from following through with their dreams is fear. Incapacitating fear can be intense and acute in response to certain situations or fear can be slow and prolonged. Both kinds of fear will probably appear at some point during your experience phase (if you don't experience fear you probably aren't being daring enough), feel free to use the Bene Gesserit litany in the case of acute or prolonged fear. In my experience the litany is most effective in the case of more acute fear, but test it out for yourself.

"Discipline Equals Freedom" - Jocko Willink Navy Seal Commander. Jocko Willink developed his concept of discipline through years of service in the Navy Seals, intense physical conditioning and through martial arts training. Understanding the importance of self-discipline doesn't come naturally to a lot of people. Many people are initially turned off by the word and the concept of discipline. The word itself seems to strike a sense of some other person imposing their will on you, but what Jocko is preaching couldn't be any more different.

Here is my own interpretation of Jocko's philosophy on discipline and why it is the best path to freedom. If you don't discipline yourself, someone else, or an external force will discipline you instead. In a financial sense, if you are disciplined with your money, i.e. you save and make smart choices, you will quickly be in a state of financial freedom. On the other hand, if you aren't disciplined with your money you will get into financial trouble and end up doing things you don't want to do to get out of your hole.

In a physical sense, if you are disciplined with your exercise and diet you will have the physical freedom to pursue whatever activities you want to pursue. If you aren't disciplined with your health, you will gradually become more and more limited in terms of you what you are capable of doing physically. People who are disciplined with their work have more freedom in terms of which jobs they can take on. So why is discipline important for people in their experience phase?

1. You need to be disciplined to maintain the other aspects of your life (finances, health, family, career, etc.)
2. Sometimes discipline is required to make certain experiences happen. For example, climbing a huge mountain is a lot of work, not to mention the training that goes into it.

I was lucky enough to discover the power of self-discipline through intense meditation and other altered states of consciousness in my late adolescence. While I certainly won't claim to be nearly as disciplined as Jocko Willink (or many other admirable people), I have been developing my own discipline for the last 8 years. At some point in the future I might write an entire book about improving self-discipline. Many psychologists have argued convincingly that discipline is a muscle, just like a muscle it needs to be trained and developed over time. I took this concept of discipline as a muscle literally and developed my own strategy for improving discipline based on scientific strength training principles.

Before going any further I want to note that the mantras I am recommending are not a substitute for strong habits and self-discipline. They will help you in your experience phase and in other aspects of your life. They are a supplement, a bonus on top of what you are already doing. An excellent time to use a mental cheat code is when your discipline is about to cave or when you know that you are about to make the wrong decision, the mantra will give you that extra boost needed to help you make the right choice. Other times the mental cheat codes will appear randomly in your mind at just the right time, in this case you got lucky and the cheat code will carry you to your goal without a substantial amount of effort on your part. Either way, mantras are a powerful tool in your toolbox.

Mindset Principles for the Experience Phase

As I said, mental cheat codes won't take you all the way there, you still need to have the right overall mentality. While I could have possibly expressed some of this additional discussion in mantra form, I believe that you will learn the concepts more deeply if I express them through different means. It is important to remember that you aren't learning facts, instead this is a different kind of knowledge, an emotional knowledge. You don't want to just believe these things at a rational analytical level, you also want this be knowledge at an emotional level and also in your deeper subconscious.

In the beginning you may take it in as factual knowledge, but over time, through contemplation and experience, I hope that you will reach a point where these thoughts become second nature to you. You don't have to accept everything that I say, instead pick and choose the information which resonates with you, then try it out and see if it works in practice.

Chase Fear and Excitement

The first principle is to seek out anything which scares and excites you at the same time (except for very risky things). The best way to orient yourself during an experience phase is to find the thing that inspires both fear and excitement. These are the emotions that occur before you exit your comfort zone. Some people have a very good sense of where their comfort zone starts and where it ends, other people are less introspective in that regard. That is where this principle comes into play. Even if you feel like you understand your own comfort zone well, consider using this technique. Throughout the course of your experience phase your comfort zone will change and expand. Even if you understand your comfort zone now, you might not understand your comfort zone after 6 months or a year of radical change.

Essentially the idea is to chase discomfort like it is your job. Go into a direction you normally wouldn't go and do things that make you feel insecure. When you find something that makes you feel insecure do it until you are comfortable. If you find something which you are bad at, this is actually a good thing, it means that you found something about yourself which you can improve. Embrace the beginner's mind.

Flow: the Optimal Experience

When you are trying something new it is ideal to not worry if you are doing it well or how you look doing it. It is best to be completely absorbed in the task. This is easier said than done. According to Psychologist Mihaly Csikszentmihalyi, flow usually occurs when you are highly skilled in an activity and are also being challenged at the same time. While I agree that this is the most likely scenario to experience a state of flow, I know that it is also possible to experience a state of total absorption in other situations. E.g. when you are doing something new and therefore have limited skills or even when you are already an expert, but aren't sufficiently challenged. On the other hand, it is also possible to be very skilled, very challenged, and also not experience flow. This is when a pro basketball player has a bad day.

While certain environmental factors can make flow more or less likely, flow can occur in any situation. Note: I don't mean to misrepresent Csikszentmihalyi's position, I believe that he would agree with most of what I said. Ultimately, the point I am trying to make, is that you can be in a state of complete absorption doing anything. And that this is the ideal state during your experience phase. If you lose your state of flow, don't be too hard on yourself, relax, take a deep breath, and try to reenter the state.

If you are unable to get into flow here is a great alternative. **Pay attention to everything around you.** Pay attention to your sights, smells, tastes, the things you hear. Pay attention to what people are saying when you are talking to them, you can learn a lot from everyone you meet if you really listen carefully to what they have to say. Pay attention to the physical sensations in your body, the tingling sensations in your fingertips, your posture, the way your leg shakes unconsciously. If you can't get into flow because of persistent thoughts, pay attention to those thoughts. You will be amazed at what you can discover if you simply pay attention.

The Fear of Missing Out

The experience phase is an amazing opportunity to go out and pursue everything you ever wanted to do. But, it is important to not get wrapped up in FOMO (The fear of missing out). In the modern age of social media and the internet in general FOMO is so common that it has become a widely used acronym. What does FOMO have to do with social media? Simple, we are constantly inundated with images, videos, and other media which depicts **highlight reel** moments and doesn't show the associated struggles, boredom and failures.

For example, look up some people in YouTube/Instagram fitness. Not only do these people have the best bodies in the world, they take pictures when they look their best, use perfect angles/lighting, and have all kinds of other techniques to represent themselves in the best possible way. Even if they try to communicate the amount of work required to achieve their amazing physiques, it is impossible to properly demonstrate years of repetition and boredom in a 30-second Instagram clip.

This problem of highlight reels isn't just in fitness, it is common all over the internet. Look up travel vlogs, sports, even those videos where people build incredible things in time-lapse. These videos might be entertaining and maybe even inspiring, the challenge is to make sure that you aren't developing unrealistic perceptions of what is possible or feeling like you have to do certain things because you keep seeing other people doing those things online.

Remember that the highlight reel doesn't represent the years of struggle and all the people who failed along the way. While there might be a few highlight reel moments in your life, chances are it will be much more ordinary most of the time. When traveling, for example, yes you see all kinds of beautiful places, but you also spend a lot of time on buses, planes, in line ups, or trying to sleep on uncomfortable beds. However, this isn't specific to traveling. Nothing in life matches up to the highlight reel.

There is another effect of highlight reel media which is possibly even more sinister. It causes us to underestimate the potential profundity of our own experiences. **Something which might seem dull on Instagram could be unbelievably transformative in our own lives.** Think about how you felt moving out of your parents' house for the first time, I bet it was a profound experience. But, can you imagine watching highlight reel photos/videos of people moving out of their parents' houses on Instagram? It sounds silly.

This is how highlight reel media gives us the impression that our own lives need to be unique to be worth living. The reality is that experiences which might seem mundane to someone else can and will be incredibly important for you in your life. You want to choose experiences based on how important they will be for you, not based on how they would appear on a highlight reel.

Don't Let Your Identity Control You

I am a firm believer in the idea that we are a collection of different entities, selves, personalities programs whatever you want to call them. These selves all coalesce to produce a single being, which is the greater you. Interestingly, you can experience life as any of these selves at any given time, some of these selves exist below the level of awareness and can be accessed through introspection. The identity is a self (or perhaps a collection of selves) which can help and hinder us. It's primary function is to keep us going in a single direction. This can be very useful if we need to be single minded for a particular task, but if we are trying something new or making drastic changes we may need to go against the desires of our identity.

During the experience phase it is important to weaken the identity, reduce its power, and make it more flexible. Some people naturally have a flexible identity, these people may have problems in other aspects of their lives, but they will thrive during their experience phase. On the other hand, if you have a stronger identity, you may struggle a bit more during your experience phase. At this point in your life your identity needs to be flexible.

The identity is not the enemy. If you, your greater self, were an organization of different people, your identity would be a very important person in that organization. Many people make their identity the CEO of their mind, and this is usually a bad idea. The identity has an agenda, it wants you to stay the same. The goal at this point in life is to experiment and experience, so your identity can't have a leadership role in your organization.

New experiences don't necessarily make you happy, they might make you happy, but they also might also cause severe pain and suffering. Often this suffering is the work of the identity. Your identity uses happiness and suffering as a way to control you. Unfortunately, most people are addicted to happiness, they allow their identities to control them.

Don't be attached to happiness and try your best to be indifferent to suffering. Otherwise your identity calls the shots. Your identity wants your dreams to stay dreams, it doesn't want you to act them out in reality. Don't chase positive emotion and don't be afraid of negative emotion. This is why people waste their money on fancy cars and expensive clothing. It feeds their identity as a wealthy person. Then they have to work harder to earn that money again so they can buy more expensive things and the cycle continues.

Say Yes

When I was 20 years old I went to visit my uncle in New York City, I have learnt a lot from him since I was a toddler. This time in New York City I asked him if he had one piece of advice he would give himself as a 20 year old. I don't remember exactly what he said, but it was something along the lines of "If someone gives you an opportunity and you aren't sure whether or not you want to do it, just say yes." Essentially err on the side of saying yes to things. This has served me a lot over the years.

I can remember being offered a job at my company's office in Germany. I wasn't sure if I wanted to go. A lot of people at my company had told me that the office in Germany is in the middle of nowhere and that there is nothing to do. On the other hand, I had always wanted to work abroad and it sounded like an awesome opportunity to earn some money and learn German. I decided to follow the principle, err on the side of yes.

I am so glad I decided to go to Germany. First off it was the best job I ever had, you often get treated better when you go abroad for your company. Second it wasn't a boring area at all, quite the opposite. I was working in the Allgäu region of Southern Germany, 2 hours west of Munich, 1 hour out of Switzerland and 20 minutes out of Austria. I worked contractually, 1-2 months on and 2-3 months traveling. But, even when I was in Germany I got to enjoy myself. I met all sorts of interesting German people who I normally wouldn't get a chance to meet as a tourist. I was working in a rural area, so as you might expect people were very friendly. While I was there I also had many opportunities to travel around Europe on my days off and I got to hike throughout the alps more times than I can count.

The reason why I am telling you this isn't simply to recount my awesome time in Germany, instead I am trying to illustrate the importance of saying yes. Sometimes it was a hard job, I had a lot of 60-80 hour workweeks, but my desire to travel and my willingness to put in the extra effort is why I got this opportunity. If you are competent, diligent, and know how to say yes at the right time, opportunities will fall on your lap.

Be Bold

Err on the side of boldness. Similar to the previous principle, not sure what to do? Choose the boldest action. In my own experience the most straightforward example is starting up conversations with strangers. While it varies depending on the culture you are in, generally speaking, everyone is at least a little bit nervous starting up a conversation with a stranger. We might worry that they won't like us, we might worry that we will say something stupid, or we might worry that they have something important to do and we don't want to annoy them. All of these are realistic possibilities and if you approach a lot of strangers they will probably all happen quite often. Err on the side of boldness and don't be afraid to fail.

This principle of boldness doesn't just apply to starting up conversations with strangers, it also applies to trying something completely new like performing live music for the first time or traveling to a completely new part of the world. Personally I have never performed live, but my understanding is that when you are performing, the bolder you are the more comfortable you appear. At least it seems that way as a spectator. In traveling, the bolder you are, so long as you don't harm yourself, the more you will get out of your experience.

I think that some people have this idea that effort should be applied to your job, school, community projects or other "serious" things and that experiences are less important and should be purely for pleasure. This is inaccurate. First off, a certain amount of effort actually makes activities more enjoyable and secondly for many people their experiences are actually more important than their job or school. If you really want to have the most interesting experiences possible it is important get serious and put in the effort.

Some experiences, like expanding your social circle, appear as effortless pure fun. Other experiences seem like a lot of work, such as hiking the Appalachian trail. However, that is just how they appear on the surface. Some people might find the social anxiety of meeting new people to be extremely effortful and other people might actually savor the grind of hiking every day. There are probably some experiences that you want to have which won't be easy, they will require commitment and persistence through challenge.

Another similar principle to follow is to **go a little bit further** every time you are getting out of your comfort zone. Going hiking? Choose the more difficult trail. Meditate a little bit longer. Write a little bit more than you feel like doing. Over time, if you keep going a little bit further than you normally would, you will expand your comfort zone further and further. Small steps add up a lot in the long run.

Your identity will use all kinds of different techniques to keep you from reinventing yourself, one of those strategies is to make you feel exhausted. Never let your identity control you, especially not in an experience phase. If you realize what it is trying to do, your identity will lose its power.

Reintegration

When you have a new experience, especially a life-changing transformative experience, it can take you some time to reintegrate. At first you might struggle with going back to your normal day-to-day activities. This isn't always the case, sometimes the new experience inspires and motivates you. Instead of struggling to do basic things like go to work, clean your house, pay your bills etc. You feel like you have endless energy for these tasks. But, other times, the transformative experience encapsulates your thoughts and makes doing other things a chore. This is part of the reason why we have an experience phase and also why we try to maintain the other parts of our life.

During these moments of reintegration, when you don't feel like doing the boring things, it is absolutely necessary to do the bare minimum necessary to maintain. Keep hitting the gym, keep showing up on time for work, keep talking to your friends and family etc. If you maintain when you don't feel like it, you will come back much stronger when you do actually feel like it.

It's very easy to be motivated when things are going well, but it is even more important to be disciplined and go through the motions when you aren't feeling it. Some people will integrate experiences more quickly than others, and some people will integrate certain kinds of experiences more quickly than others. Make sure to always give yourself more than enough time to integrate and understand how long it takes you to get back on course. Later on in this book I will explain what to do when the experience phase is over, but even during the phase it is important to reorient yourself. This is where habits like meditation, journaling, sleep, and fitness are valuable.

Always Make Risk Assessments

The next principle is to always make risk assessments. I don't want you reading this book, deciding that you are going to have an experience phase, and messing up your life because of some stunt you try to do. I have said this before, but I will keep repeating it, **being in an experience phase doesn't make you invulnerable**, you can still get hurt badly. For some people this won't a problem at all, perhaps you are good at assessing risk. Other people, those who tend to get wrapped up in excitement, will have more problems. One good trick is to think of someone who is very rational and ask yourself what they would do in the situation. This should keep you from doing something unsafe. Don't risk your health or finances, instead choose to risk looking foolish or making a silly mistake.

See your Emotions for what they really are

The way to stop chasing emotions is to see them for what they are, an illusion. Like a shadow when you shine a light on an emotion it goes away. I discovered this one day on an empty beach in British Columbia Canada. Despite being November in Canada, it was a beautiful day, so I decided to walk to the beach. I was 19 years old and had just gotten into meditation. At the time I knew how much fear and anxiety controlled my life, but I didn't think that it was possible to do anything about that. My fears and anxieties felt like a chain I couldn't escape from.

While meditating at the beach I started to experience an intense fear. I wasn't afraid of anything in particular, it was more of a general sense of fear. Instead of shying away from that fear as I usually did, I decided to go into it and to understand what it is. I looked more closely, and I experienced the fear in the most intense and profound way possible. My fear appeared in my mind's eye as flashing lights, then it transformed into a tunnel. After going into the tunnel I was launched forward and experienced the most intense fear imaginable, but somehow the experience was ecstatic because that fear was also paired with an equivalent sense of courage. I continued to fly forward faster and faster and I kept asking for more. I'm not sure how much time passed, but eventually I had one of the most profound experiences of my life, I realized that my fear was an illusion, it didn't even exist. All I had to do was to go into it.

Now I realize that this applies to all the emotions that we experience, including happiness. Notice how you stop experiencing happiness once you realize that you are feeling happy. All emotions are a dream and it is possible to wake up. But, this knowledge doesn't grant you effortless freedom from your emotions. I still regularly find myself beholden to my identity, doing things that I otherwise wouldn't want to do because my identity is controlling me through a carrot or a stick. But, on numerous occasions, my knowledge of the nature of my emotions allowed me to make the best decisions of my life. Note: when you first focus on an emotion it may magnify and become more intense, if it is an unpleasant emotion continue to focus on it and ask for more until it disappears.

Ego Death

The experience phase will likely result in one or many ego-deaths. Ego-death is a fairly elusive concept and people use it in all kinds of different ways. I will give my own definition for the purpose of this book. Ego-death is an experience which shatters your identity and as a result completely transforms your sense of who you are. It turns out, many things that we believe are fundamental about ourselves, are actually just inventions of our identity. The beauty of ego-death is that it shows us who we are beneath our sense of identity. This is the ultimate experience in finding yourself. It should go without saying that you will need a long time to reintegrate after an ego-death.

Actually any identity change that you experience is a result of a mini ego-death plus reintegration afterwards. By experiencing something new you challenge your identity, "kill" that part of your identity, and are reborn into something new. The term ego-death, in all of its glory, is usually reserved for the most profound "ego-deaths", but it can also be used in more ordinary situations. Note: I think it should be called "identity death" instead of ego death. The word ego has come to be associated with a sense of superiority or arrogance, but in the context of ego-death it actually has a different meaning. In this context it is referring to your sense of self. Yes an ego-death experience may be humbling, but it could also have the opposite effect. Your identity might reintegrate into something awful, ego-death is not necessarily a good or a bad thing.

I should be clear that the **identity is not the enemy**. Actually your identity is very important in certain situations. Many people notice that once they have children they are suddenly able to focus and live their lives in a more serious way, this is an example of when our identities are invaluable. When we have some kind of important responsibility. Imagine if a president or prime minister suddenly had an ego-death and no longer felt like a president, or if a mother suddenly decided that she no longer felt like a mother because of a deep self-realization. Identity is in many ways the foundation of modern civilization and it forms the structure of how we all operate as humans on a day-to-day basis. Through all this conversation about identity I am not trying to make you detest your identity or attempt to kill it completely, I am simply showing you how it can in some instances prevent you from thriving.

***

I suggest making a habit of **writing every single day** during your experience phase. I started journaling regularly during my intellectual phase and continued this habit into my experience phase. The awesome thing about writing is that it serves as a reminder of how you were feeling at a particular moment in time. If you don't write during your experience phase you will probably still remember the things that you did, but you almost certainly won't remember what you were thinking or feeling on a day-to-day basis. This is where journaling comes in. You will now have a record of everything going on in your mind and the things that you were doing from every single day in your life.

When I think back to periods in my life where I didn't write anything down I can remember certain things, but most of it is a blur. When I review journal entries from times in my life when I was writing every day I start to remember all kinds of other things that I didn't even write down. I know that if I wasn't journaling there are tons of important events and ideas in my life that I would forget completely. Probably it doesn't really matter if you journal, what matters is that you produce something every day to remind yourself what you were up to. Trust me, you will be grateful that you did it in the future. It would probably be fine to use voice or video logs as well, or anything else which expresses your thoughts and feelings in a sufficiently descriptive way.

My own habit of journaling gradually evolved into writing for other people and that eventually resulted in this book. When I started writing I didn't originally intend on ever showing anyone else my work, but now writing for other people has become one of my main passions.

Some people find that buying a beautiful journal helps motivate them to actually write. While I think that this is a great idea I have come to rely on more bland notebooks simply because I go through journals so quickly. It makes more sense to get a cheap notebook if you are going to need to buy a new one in two weeks. But, most people don't go through notebooks that quickly so it might more sense for you to buy a new one, at least to motivate yourself in the beginning.

When should you Commit to something?

Commitment is an interesting question during an experience phase. You might feel like you don't want to commit to anything because that will prevent you from experiencing other things, but on the other hand certain experiences require a substantial amount of commitment. Here is a very silly example which plagues a lot of travelers. People will feel overwhelmed by all the different countries that they can visit. They might have saved up a substantial amount of money and are in a perfect situation to travel the world, but they always feel like they are going to the wrong country because they have so many other options. Don't let this get in your way.

Yes, it is a good idea to evaluate all of the possibilities, but once you made your choice focus on that. As an example, if you go to Thailand it is so easy to look at all the cheap flights to the nearby countries. It might only cost 50 dollars to fly to Vietnam or 100 dollars to fly to the Philippines. But, make sure to enjoy your time in Thailand until it comes time to visit another country. And when it comes to travel as well as having any other experience don't be afraid to make a commitment. The experience phase is not anti-commitment so long as those commitments don't completely tie you down and prevent you from living the life that you want to live. Note: the experience phase itself is a huge commitment, especially if your experience phase lasts for a few years or more.

11
Guiding Someone Else

Most of this book is for people who actually want to have an experience phase, but it is very possible that you know someone else who is thinking about having an experience phase themselves. This chapter is for parents, spouses, siblings, coaches/counsellors, and close friends who want the best for "the adventurer" in their life.

First Check in with Yourself

Do you truly want the best for this person? Or are you motivated by some other factor? The truth is that when many people give advice they aren't necessarily giving the best advice they possibly can, instead they are allowing their own desires and fears to cloud their thinking. Here are some of the ways that your advice can be biased.

1. You project your own desires onto the other person: Many people have things in their lives which they haven't yet done, but wish that they could do. Instead of actually going out and pursuing these dreams, they try to get someone else to pursue them so they can live vicariously through that person. Occasionally the person giving the advice is literally unable to pursue these experiences, or they simply don't have the courage.

2. You don't empathize with the other person: This is similar to the previous situation, but a tad different as well. When many people give advice they ignore the fact that the person they are giving advice to is much different from themselves. They forget that the other person has different motivations, different abilities and different weaknesses. Whenever anyone gives any kind of advice they are always partially clouded by their own biases, but that doesn't mean that it is impossible to give good advice. Just be aware of these biases and limit them as much as possible.

3. You are envious: Many people have been unable to live the life that they hoped they would live. As a result they are bitter and they try to convince other people to not live out their dreams. Most of the time this isn't a conscious malicious desire, instead it is more subconscious. Advice that comes from jealousy is usually warning the person against taking a risk. In some cases it is actually a good idea to warn them about taking a risk, but ask yourself if this warning is out of genuine concern for them or because you are threatened by their optimism.

Never pressure someone into having an experience phase. You might think that people only pressure other people to not have an experience phase, but the reverse can happen as well. Our cultural value systems are changing and people are placing more and more value on experiences and less value on things like the accumulation of material resources. My prediction is that this trend will continue and people will be feel pressured to take on an experience phase when it isn't actually the right thing for them. Remember that the experience phase is supposed to be something you do for yourself and not something to appease other people.

I can imagine someone reading this book and trying to convince everyone around them to have an experience phase, please don't do this! Sure you can tell people about the concept of an experience phase but if they don't feel like it is the right thing for them don't pressure them further. An experience phase won't bring anyone happiness and it won't solve any problems on its own. Sure experiences inform and enrich your life, but experiences can be had in a lot of different ways. All that being said, I still believe that a lot of people can and will benefit from an experience phase, if it is right for them specifically.

***

Let's say that someone in your life has decided that they want to have an experience phase. What then?

Don't pay for it!

If you are supporting them financially during their experience phase it isn't an experience phase anymore, now it is just an excuse for them to be lazy. Sure some people will take advantage of the opportunity and actually pursue a lot of the experiences that they have always dreamed of having, but a lot of other people won't have the drive necessary to live well even if they are in the perfect situation.

Ultimately, working for the experience is part of the experience itself. Whether they volunteer or get a job to support their goals it doesn't matter, what matters is that they pull their own weight somehow. If at any point they ask you for money the experience phase is over, this means that they failed and that they need to get their life on track. The one exception in terms of giving them money is if they are actually able to pull their own weight and work for you.

If you are going to support them it is better to support them emotionally or to give them specific advice, but only when they really need it. Let them do their own thing most of the time and don't butt in unless you think they are making a big mistake.

Make sure that they aren't taking any huge financial or safety risks

When assessing risk it is critical that you understand the availability heuristic. Instinctually, human beings assess risk by how many times they can recall an actual occurrence of an event. This is a widely researched and understood cognitive bias. The thing to bear in mind is that when people use the availability heuristic it is sometimes accurate, on these occasions a likely event is also an easily recalled event, but in other situations the heuristic is completely incorrect.

Many people are afraid of getting on airplanes because they are able to recall numerous instances of airplane accidents in the media, but in actuality airplanes are extremely safe. On the other hand, a lot of people text and drive despite the fact that this is an extremely dangerous activity simply because they can't recall specific instances of people dying texting and driving. A similar but slightly distinct heuristic is where someone assesses risk by how easy it is to imagine the event, there is some overlap because events can be easier to imagine if it is possible to recall specific instances.

When you think that someone is taking a huge risk ask yourself, are they really taking a big risk or does it just appear that way? In many situations they actually aren't taking that big of a risk at all. If you rationally look at the situation and decide that they are definitely taking a big risk then it is a good idea to interfere at that point.

Don't give too much Advice

Someone in an experience phase will likely have too many possible experiences on their mind to be able to pursue all of them. When you give them a bunch of different suggestions it doesn't actually help them at all, if anything it will make their life more difficult because they get overwhelmed. Plus they will not take you as seriously if you are constantly giving them new suggestions, they will just start to find you annoying.

That being said, well timed well thought out suggestions can go a long way. The best time to give a suggestion is when they ask for one. If they never ask for a suggestion a good rule of thumb is a maximum of one suggestion per year, any more than that would probably bother most people. Limiting yourself to once a year will force you to be very contemplative and careful about using your suggestion properly and the other person will take it much more seriously. One very good suggestion goes further than hundreds of terrible suggestions. It is so tempting to give people all kinds of suggestions, but are your suggestions really better than what they would do naturally? Maybe their own ideas are kind of lame and you have the best ideas ever, but chances are that they have good ideas themselves.

Now in terms of emotional support they will need encouragement that they are doing the right thing. When someone takes on an experience phase they will probably doubt that they are using their time effectively and also people around them will likely think they are a making a mistake having an experience phase. This is where your support comes in, try your best to make sure that they know that an experience is actually worth their time. You might have to continuously remind them of this fact, especially considering how many other people around them will likely be saying the opposite.

I can imagine that some parents would be a bit unsure of how to deal with their children's experiences phases. Some of them would probably be very concerned and frightened and others would be thrilled by the idea. As a caveat I have never had kids so take my advice with a grain of salt. Focus on the important issues. If your kids want to have an experience phase make sure that they don't seriously hurt themselves, hurt someone else, or lose a lot of money. And limit your suggestions to once a year (unless your kids actually ask you for suggestions). Also, get your kids a copy of this book : P

On the other hand, **never try to pressure your kids into having an experience phase** if they don't want to. Some people don't naturally seek out new experiences and there is nothing wrong with that. No one ever had to pressure me into doing it, seeking out experiences is a natural instinct. That doesn't mean that your child should sit around and do nothing, on the other hand the kid who doesn't have an inclination to pursue new experiences should focus on other parts of their life like their career or their contributions to their community. Ultimately, there is only so much you can do to influence your kids life, even if you want them to go through an experience phase it might not be the right thing for them personally.

If your **employee** wants to have an experience phase this could be a tricky situation. I was very lucky in that my employer was surprisingly understanding of my desire to travel the world, but I can imagine that many employers wouldn't have been nearly as forgiving. If they are a good employee you will probably want to keep them on the team, but on the other hand you don't want people coming and going at their own discretion.

Possibly you can find part-time work for them to do, or even give them work to do from the computer. Maybe in their particular experience phase they are able to keep a full-time job, in this situation in makes sense to avoid giving them any huge responsibilities throughout the course of their experience phase. Depending on your industry, it may be possible to offer them a sabbatical. Finally, if you don't value them as an employee or if there is no way to resolve the situation, it may make sense to let them go.

A **spouse/partner** wanting to have an experience phase is probably the trickiest situation. On the one hand we want the best for our partners, but on the other hand it can be challenging to deal with a lover going through a personal change. It is very possible that they change so much that the relationship will be over by the end of the experience phase. Throughout the course of an experience phase people discover who they are at a deeper level, and in many cases they learn that they have in fact been living a life which is incoherent with their truest selves. Perhaps the transition to their true self will be painful for the people around them, but hopefully the world as a whole will be a better place when they start living in a more honest way.

***

Sure there are other kinds of situations where you might know someone who is taking on an experience phase, but I feel like the previous examples are probably the most critical. In other situations I recommend following the advice from the rest of the chapter, make sure that they don't take any enormous physical or financial risks and limit your suggestions to one time per year.

If you are worried that the experience phase will slow down their progress in some other aspect of their life just remember that it will benefit them as a whole over the long run. Having a new experience is like buying a blue-chip stock, it returns dividends over time. Every decision that they make will be informed by that experience, it gives them additional information about the world and about themselves. Remember that a lot of people waste their time whether they are in an experience phase or not. Is it a choice between an experience phase and a fulfilling career or is it a choice between an experience phase and a lot of Netflix?

Be very Cautious before you Warn Someone not to have an Experience Phase

This is only appropriate in a few circumstances. Basically any situation where they have a tremendous degree of responsibility, for example if they have just had children or if hold an important position in the political arena. Otherwise by warning them against an experience phase you are potentially getting in the way of their only chance to live out their dreams in actuality. If an experience phase truly is a bad idea in their situation and you have no choice but to caution them against it, make sure to explain to them the consequences of their decision. Also, remind them of the future possibilities of having an experience phase later on in their life. So long as you are still alive it is never too late to have an experience phase, as I have mentioned before it is always possible to have an experience phase in retirement.

When to Step Back

It is important to know when is the right time to accompany them and when is the right time to let them do their own thing. When it comes to your children (assuming they are adults) it is probably best to let them do their own thing almost all of the time, only occasionally interfering when it absolutely necessary. Trust in their abilities, eventually they will need to make it alone anyway.

If they can't make their own decisions during their experience phase they might never learn how to make their own decisions. Probably the only time it makes sense to get involved is when they are your close friend or your spouse. In both of these cases you want to be around to the watch their progression and see if the person they are becoming is a person that you want to associate with. Either way, don't get involved too much and let them be independent most of the time.

What to do if they are taking Big Risks

You might encounter a scenario where you know someone who is taking too many risks in their experience phase, but at the same time they aren't willing to listen to your warnings. In this situation it is important to flank their ego. If you come at them head on and tell them not to do whatever they are doing wrong over and over again they will keep insisting on taking the risk (unless they really respect you). But, if you improve your relationship with them and display genuine interest in their experience phase they will likely be more receptive to your concerns.

It is better to focus on the relationship with the person and express your concerns once than it is to remind them of how dumb they are multiple times a day. As I mentioned earlier you have one suggestion per year for things to do, another good rule of thumb would be one concern per year I.e. one thing per year which you tell them not to do. If you limit yourself to one concern per year they will take it much more seriously. Also, the less you interfere the better the experience phase will be overall because an experience phase is supposed to be fundamentally independent. It's good if they make a lot of mistakes, this is how they learn. It's only a problem if they make a mistake which has serious consequences.

Naturally, the amount that you get involved in their experience phase depends a lot on what culture you are in. Some cultures are more individualistic and as a result individuals tend to carve their own life path more often. Other cultures are more collectivistic and as a consequence these cultures tend to have more predefined life paths. As a Canadian I am used to a much more individualistic culture, so I am accustomed to people carving out their own life paths. Perhaps my one suggestion a year and one concern a year rule wouldn't be appropriate in other cultures, however this is not entirely clear to me. Whichever culture you are in, an experience phase is supposed to be independent so maybe the once a year rule works everywhere.

An Example of Good Advice

There were a few times during my own experience phase when I sought out advice from other people and the advice they gave me was excellent. Early on in my travels I met an elderly German man in Honduras, he had been to all 7 continents and to 192 countries. He had travelled non-stop for the last 40 years, with 2 month breaks every year in Germany. Realizing that he had a huge store of knowledge about the world I started quizzing him on different countries and got a lot of valuable information.

I asked him to list his top 5 most interesting countries to visit, but he said that my question was impossible to answer. So instead I asked him to list 5 countries that would fit into his top 10. This was doable. He included Bolivia, India, Ethiopia, and the entire region of Central Europe. After visiting all of these places I am in complete agreement. Personally, I would include Colombia and Indonesia, but I can appreciate his recommendations as well.

On the other hand, I can't think of a single time during my experience phase where I was given unsolicited advice which was very helpful at all. People often gave me advice, but it was usually without empathy. It neglected to consider my own motivations and desires and was more a reflection of their own insecurities and/or unfulfilled dreams. Fortunately, I realized this almost every time. This is why solicited advice is so much more effective than unsolicited advice. The person asking for advice is able to form the question in such a way that the advice will be perfect for their particular situation.

Age is a factor to consider. I was 21 when I started my experience phase, which may be older or younger than the person in your life. Generally speaking, it is impossible to start an experience phase below the age of 18, however I have met a couple of 17 year olds traveling through southeast Asia, so I guess some people do start a little bit younger. Other people start their experience phase much older.

If the person is very young it will be harder to let them go out and live their own life, you will likely be more worried. If they are older you really don't have any excuse to get involved, if they can't make it on their own at this point they probably never will. Really as long as they are safe it's no big deal. In a sense the younger they are the less important it is that they make good choices. They have so much fewer responsibilities at a young age so if they screw up it doesn't matter. Compare a young adult failing a class in University to an older adult losing their job and being unable to pay their mortgage. One event is mostly irrelevant over the long-run and the other event will ruin their lives.

Encourage them to take Sensible Risks

Whenever someone decides to do something risky or out of the ordinary usually the people around them will try to convince them not to do it. In this situation you want to be the one person in their life who is pushing them to take the risk, assuming that it isn't actually a huge risk that they are taking.

As long as they aren't hurting themselves, always encourage them to go a little bit further. Think about the word (en)(courage), it literally means to imbue with courage. Often the difference between someone following through with their dreams and shying away from them is a little bit of courage. "Courage is not the absence of fear, but rather the assessment that something else is more important than fear" - Franklin D. Roosevelt. Ultimately, they have to make the decision themselves to overcome their fear, there is only so much you can do. But, you can and should try your best to give them a little boost.

If they want to go skydiving encourage them to do it, this is a low-risk activity but it invokes fear in a lot of people. Be the guiding force that helps them overcome their fear at the appropriate time. As long as they aren't acting irrationally, more courage is always better.

There is a subtle art to helping people understand their own strengths and weaknesses. With some people you can straight up tell them what you think and occasionally people will even ask for your opinion, but with others you will need be more indirect with the hints. Either way it just as important to remind them that these strengths and weaknesses are simply their current condition and that their actual limits are undefined. Remind them that they can improve any aspect of their life substantially, all they have to do is focus and put in the required work.

As I mentioned in previous chapters, **maintenance is a key part of the experience phase.** If their career, family life, or health is deteriorating you may need to step in. Don't step in too early, reserve this for critical situations when you see potential for long-term damage. As is the case with other forms of unrequested help, interfering too often can and will strain the relationship. But, if they are ignoring major aspects of their life it may be necessary that you step in, they will probably thank you in the future.

    Closing this chapter I should mention that it is critical that you question your own motives for trying to influence someone else's experience phase. Do you really want the best for them or is this just wish fulfillment? Have you had your own experience phase? And if not, why not? If you are trying to help them know themselves better, have you first taken the time to know yourself? Many people who are constantly giving other people advice and giving other people suggestions are not taking their own advice. On airplanes they tell you to put on your own mask first. Before you try to help someone else make sure that your own life is in order.

12
What Next?

What to do after your experience phase? The first thing to decide is whether or not you are going to have another dedicated phase. I suggest taking some time to decide how you are going to spend the next couple of years. I decided on my own dedicated phases after moments of inspiration, but these "moments" of inspiration were preceded by long periods of deliberation. While I wasn't consciously thinking about what I should do for my next dedicated phase, I was often thinking about the nature of my own life. Even if I wasn't consciously aware of it, I believe that my subconscious mind was often processing the question of what my next dedicated phase should be about.

There are a number of different dedicated phases that you could have. In this chapter I am going to list some of the more standard options. Bear in mind that I have only personally gone through an Intellectual Phase and an Experience Phase, so much of my advice doesn't come from my own experience, instead it comes from my observations and conversations with other people. Interpret what I say with caution.

Career/Financial Phase

The first option and probably a good option for a lot of people after their experience phase would be a career/financial phase. After a few months or even a few years experiencing new things most people will have a good idea of who they are and what they want to do with their lives. The career/financial phase is a smart idea for people who feel like they need to put more energy into their careers.

Are you always having money problems? Or are you insecure about your lack of success in business? If so you are a good candidate for a career phase. This phase is characterized by working much longer hours, saving lots of money by avoiding unnecessary purchases, and taking risks if necessary. Of course, just like an experience phase, it is still important to maintain the other aspects of your life.

The length of a career/financial phase will depend on your specific goals, how much money you have saved up, and how far along you already are in your career. Someone who has a well-established career could potentially make major headway in only a couple of years. But, someone who has never had a real job and doesn't have much in the bank could take as long as 10 years (or more) to get where they want to be. Either way, the career/financial phase usually takes longer than some of the other phases.

Family Phase

The next option, which is also a great choice for a lot of people after an experience phase, would be a family phase. By family I am not referring to the family you already have, instead I am referring to having children. Naturally, this isn't an option or even a desire for a lot of people. Having a family is another long phase, possibly the longest phase in your life.

Spiritual Phase

Another good option would be a spiritual phase. Many people, myself included, put their spiritual phase into their experience phase. However, these phases might be distinct for you. There are numerous different religions and spiritualities so I want to limit my discussion by avoiding specific recommendations. I could go through my own particular meditation process, but I actually don't think that it is necessarily superior to other methods. If you have no interest in spirituality and no background in religion I still recommend some kind of spiritual path. People vary in their need for spiritual experiences, but I think it is something that almost everyone needs at some level.

One good thing about a spiritual phase is that it can be as short as a couple of months, but for some people their spiritual phase lasts 10 years or more. Some people even stay on the spiritual path their entire lives. My personal spiritual development actually started during my intellectual phase and persisted through my experience phase. Currently, I maintain the things I discovered during that time by meditating every single morning. Don't feel like your spiritual phase needs to be glamorous or adventurous, it could be as simple as studying the Bible or the Talmud, but if you feel inclined to do something more audacious then go for it!

Responsibility Phase

Another sort of dedicated phase you could consider having would be a responsibility phase. This is a period of time where you dedicate yourself to meeting your ethical and moral obligations (or at least putting yourself in a position to meet your ethical and moral obligations). It's not necessarily about taking on more responsibilities, although it could be in some situations, instead the responsibility phase is about fulfilling the responsibilities you feel that you have in your own life.

My own personal belief is that people are ethically obligated to at least in part support their family, community, and the greater human race so long as they are capable of supporting themselves. I am not implying that people are obligated to sacrifice for others, actually I believe that our primary ethical duty is towards supporting ourselves, but once we are more than capable of supporting ourselves it makes sense to divert some of our energy into supporting other people and the institutions which keep our societies functioning.

Some people will never reach that point where they are entirely self-sufficient, these people will spend their entire lives relying on other people, but our societies require that at least some people take responsibility for everyone else.

Your Own Idea

When it comes to planning out your own life and applying the dedicated phase concept feel free to make up your own phases. These previous phases were just some ideas that I came up with, but modifying any of my phases or even coming up with something completely different might work better for you personally.

Here are some principles to follow when you are coming up with your own phase.

1. Choose something which benefits from a concentrated effort. An experience phase or a financial phase benefit from the extreme focus that the dedicate phase allows. On the other hand, a relationship phase could possibly be a bad idea simply because the intense focus might destroy the relationship(s) themselves.

2. Choose an aspect of your life which needs work and doesn't seem to be improving on its own. For example if you don't have healthy habits a year-long fitness/health phase could put you into a position where you are able to maintain those healthy habits for the rest of your life. In every situation (and in this example in particular) it is always important to maintain your strong position when the phase is over.

General (Maintenance) Phase

Another option to consider would be not having a dedicated phase at all. Normally, this is a good idea for a few months or a year at the most. However, a small number of people can operate throughout their entire lives in a "general" phase. This works much better for certain people than it does for other people. Most of us make little to no progress in a general phase and are better served focusing on one thing at a time. A big advantage of having a general phase after your experience phase is that it will allow you to take care of anything that broke down. You could characterize this shorter General Phase as a Maintenance Phase.

While I say it is important to maintain the other aspects of your life during your experience phase, probably something will breakdown at least a little bit. This short general phase is useful because it will allow you to rebuild any aspects of your life which broke down during the experience phase, a few months should be long enough if you maintained everything reasonably well. It will also be useful to have a general phase if you can't decide which phase to have after your experience phase. After the short general phase you should have a better understanding of which aspects of your life need more work or what kind of phase you feel like having.

Transitioning to the Next Phase

Moving from one stage in your life to the next stage can be a difficult process. Inevitably there will be a pain period while you adapt to new habits. Some people will find it more painful than others, this depends on how high they score on the Big Five sub-trait orderliness. Conscientious, one of the main Big Five traits, can be split up into orderliness and industriousness. Orderliness is characterized by the following qualities.

- Need for structure
- Preference for organization
- Punctuality
- Tidiness
- Disgust sensitivity

People who are high in orderliness depend on their routines and struggle to deal with change in their lives. People who are lower in orderliness on the other hand tend to be much more flexible and are able to adapt to new circumstances. While there are a lot of advantages to being high in orderliness, someone who is higher in orderliness will usually struggle with a phase change in their life. If you are very orderly you need to embrace the chaotic side within you during a phase change. Your orderliness is your strength, but at this particular point it becomes your weakness.

People who are high in orderliness will thrive after a year or more in a particular phase. They struggle to change their habits, but once they have a structured routine they really get into their element. People like me who are more chaotic struggle to maintain a routine. Deep in my different life phases I have had to find ways to stay stimulated, if you are very low in orderliness even a small change can increase your enthusiasm for life. On the other hand, no matter how chaotic your personality there is always some degree of order inside of you. It is important for us to embrace this order and learn to use it at the right time.

Understand where you fit on the chaos-order spectrum, learn to embrace your strengths and recognize your weaknesses. Understand that there is tremendous value in both ways of being and be aware of the potential pitfalls of your own personality. While I am very high on the chaos end of the spectrum I still have a lot of respect for people who are more orderly. Perhaps you are somewhere in the middle, in this case you will probably have both the strengths and weaknesses of orderly and chaotic people.

If you are struggling during a phase change and it feels like it is taking you too long to adapt use this mantra **"life is not about maturing quickly, it is about maturing well."** Many people, in western cultures particularly, feel like they need to progress through each life stage as fast as possible. I can remember wanting to finish University in 3 years by taking summer courses, this ended up being an overly ambitious goal. In retrospect I would have been better off doing the opposite and taking a few years off school before University to work full-time and understand myself better, but at the time I felt like this was a form of failure.

In a sense, **the more challenging your phase change the better.** This gives you more opportunities to learn about yourself. Don't rush through the pain of the phase change or try to ignore it altogether. Observe the pain, savor it, and it will naturally subside. If you are able to detach from your emotions and recognize that they aren't you, you will be able to graduate into your next phase with dignity.

This chapter is just as much about moving on from the experience phase as it is about moving on from any particular phase in your life. The process of moving from one phase to another is often tricky, but the lessons you learn moving on from your experience phase will apply to other phase changes as well. Embrace the phase change as an opportunity to learn, any painful experience can be made more tolerable by framing it at as a learning experience.

Not only will you learn strategies that help you process phase changes, but you will also learn more about how well you deal with change itself. Test yourself to see how well you are able to handle the transition. Remember the transition can last anywhere from a few months to longer than a year, watch how you respond to a changing environment.

Because of my temperament I often experience a boost in productivity and enthusiasm right after a major life change. However, just like everyone else, I do experience some growing pains during phase changes.

If you are higher in orderliness recognize that you will experience more pain and resistance during this period. Don't worry if your phase change is difficult, it may take you months or even more than a year to fully adapt. You will probably notice all kinds of habits from your experience phase popping up at surprising moments during your next phase. You can get rid of these habits over time or keep them if you want. It will only take a very small effort to maintain these habits, just make it a conscious effort occasionally.

Any phase change in life will result in an ego-death of sorts. In some cases this ego-death will be dramatic and completely life changing, in other situations the ego-death will be much more minor. This is why the transition is painful, your identity is trying to keep you from changing. But, it is better to go through the pain of a phase change than it is to get stuck in an experience phase for your entire life. Don't shy away from pain, this is how your identity controls you. Human beings are born addicted to happiness, if we can transcend this addiction we can transcend our animal nature. When you no longer chase happiness and avoid pain you are free to live as you choose.

A new phase is a time in your life when you experience fear, excitement, and discomfort all at the same time. It is like a new experience, but on a much larger scale. Personally, I get more excited by the prospect of a new life phase than I do about any particular experience. While you will probably be experiencing some pain, you might also be experiencing even more anticipation, excitement, and hope about your future.

Moving on

Some people will feel the desire to continue their experience phase indefinitely. This is the tendency any time we are moving from one phase to another, but it may be even stronger for people who particularly value new experiences or for people who had an enlightening experience phase. But, it is important to stay committed to the time frame you originally set out for yourself before you started the experience phase.

Remember, ending your experience phase doesn't mean that your life will suddenly become boring. While you might not have as many new exciting experiences as you used to have, you will now have more meaningful goals and of course you should always be pursuing new experiences at least some of the time (depending on your temperament). As a matter of fact the new experiences that you have after your experience phase may feel even more intense because you will be more sensitive.

One of the effects of the experience phase is that you become desensitised to new experiences and they don't affect you as much. This is a benefit in the sense that it allows you to emotionally deal with more intense experiences in a shorter amount of time, but it is a downside in the fact that you might not remember those experiences as well.

In your next phase you simply won't be having as many new experiences so they will affect you much more. When you are having some new wild experience during your next phase it will have a greater impact simply because it will feel more intense.

Set Realistic Phase Goals

When you plan your next dedicated phase make sure that it is not only something that you want to do, but also something you could realistically pull off. Many people make huge plans for their life, but don't take into account the reality of how difficult it will be to follow through with that plan. When I began my experience phase I was only 21 years old, at the time I knew that if I planned out a 5-year experience phase I would finish at 26, which is still very young. Although it was a bit challenging to follow through at certain times, it wasn't overly ambitious. I think if I had decided on a 10-year experience phase ending at 31 years old, I might have not been able to follow through.

So make sure that you not only understand your ambitions, but also have a deep understanding of your limitations. There is another factor which is that it is nearly impossible to know how you will feel in the very long run. Personally, I prefer to plan in 5-7 year windows because it is very hard to predict how my values will change past the 5-7 year mark. 10 years could be a reasonable number for some people. Probably the older you are the more realistically you can plan longer into the future.

Some People will try to hold you back

The next challenge you will experience moving onto your next life phase will be from the people around you. Remember how other people reacted when you started your experience phase? You will get the same resistance moving out of your experience phase. People will have become attached to that former version of you, the person who travelled the world or the surf bum who chased the endless summer. Let's say you want to have a family phase, but have been living out of a van for the last 5 years climbing mountains. Here are some of the different kinds of resistance you will experience from people around you.

1. People won't believe that you will actually be able to change. They have placed you into the category of the wild girl who doesn't live seriously and chases fun. The truth is that if you commit to a change you can become a completely new person, but some people close to you won't see that. The trick to overcoming the people who doubt you is not to cut them out of your life entirely, instead when they imply that you won't be able to transition to your next phase simply smile, thank them for the input, and do whatever you were planning on doing anyway.

2. People will also resist your transformation because it threatens their understanding of the world. Their conception of the world includes the fact that people can't radically change their personality. They have some conception of who you are and through your transformation you threaten this idea that people can't change. Maybe they have the idea that people can't change because of some experience they had with their parents or maybe they hold onto this idea because of some weakness that they never got rid of. This isn't necessarily conscious on their part, instead it is the work of their identity working in alliance with your identity to keep you from transforming. Don't let your identities cooperate, simply don't allow their doubts to hold serious weight in your mind.

While some people will try to keep you from changing, other people will support your transition. These are likely the same people who supported you during the beginning of the experience phase, but not necessarily. Some people value experiences above all else and will try to keep you in the experience phase for your entire life. Other people value other phases and will try to keep you in that phase for your entire life. But, still some people will support you to improve and transform no matter what.

Interestingly, **all of these people are important in your life**. Change isn't always a good thing, in some cases it is better to keep going in the same direction. But, in this particular scenario you are following through with a previous commitment which is ending your experience phase after a particular amount of time. So in this situation it is critical to actually follow through with the change and ignore the people who are trying to keep you in your experience phase. These sorts of people are valuable during the experience phase and in other points in your life so don't cut them out completely, just recognize that their input should be ignored right now.

Find the people who are supporting your transition and spend more time with them. At this point in your life these people are invaluable because they will help you deal with the challenges and emotional stress of moving from one phase to the next. Once you have settled into your next phase you can go back to spending a lot of time with the people who doubted your ability to transition, they will eventually accept the new version of you.

You might want to cut them out completely for doubting you or giving you bad advice. But it is better to keep them around. It's not easy to make good friends. Some of us know tons of different people, but hardly anyone has a lot of close friends. The way I see it, someone isn't really a close friend until you have known them for years. No one is perfect. When you move from one phase to another it might produce a lot of negative reactions from some of the people around you, but that doesn't mean that you should end the relationship. Continue to occasionally stay in touch with them and maintain the friendship/family bond. Even if they upset you somehow, recognize that people are valuable in different situations. You never want to completely lose touch with a close friend or family member unless they become absolutely intolerable or destructive.

Chaos and Order

Fundamentally, this book is about how and when to embrace change (chaos). But, order is just as important. When you move on to your next phase you will gradually develop a new order and organization in your life. Most self-help books are about creating order so I decided to write a book which focuses on those times in your life when you need to accept a certain degree of chaos.

Chaos might have a negative connotation, but a destruction of order is necessary to create new order. As you move from one phase to another your identity will need to be partially destroyed in order to create the new identity in your next phase. Chaos is an inevitable result of this destruction.

Accepting Phase Changes

A lot of the major problems that people experience in their lives are due to them not being willing to accept phase changes. This happens at every single phase change in life starting in early childhood.

1. Some children, when they enter into elementary school, have trouble adapting to the new lifestyle. These children are attached to their home life and don't want to accept their new identity as a student. In Kindergarten, I can remember seeing my mom and my brother playing in the playground at my school, I literally ran away from class to go play with them. My teacher didn't even notice until my mom took me back to class. The concepts I describe in this book may be challenging for a young child to understand, but they will be helpful for a parent who is trying to empathize with their child.

2. A classic example of someone who is unwilling to move on from a previous identity is uncle Rico from the cult film Napoleon Dynamite. In case you haven't seen the movie uncle Rico is a has been high school football star who believes his coach held him back from becoming a professional football player. Despite being middle-aged uncle Rico is still obsessed with his high school success and missed opportunities. Many people are attached to their

high school years and struggle to move onto the next stage in their lives.

3. Young adults often struggle with basic responsibilities. This is in part because they are unwilling to accept the fact that they are no longer children and now must take on the identity of an adult. Part of the reason why they try to stay children is because they are simply lazy, but the main reason is due to identity. They simply don't want to accept their new role in society as an adult.

4. Retirees have a similar problem where their identity has become so wrapped up in their work that when it comes time to stop working they struggle to find new meaning in their lives. It seems like people who find something engaging to do after retirement actually live longer than people who remain attached to their previous job.

5. Nearly everyone who has a break up after a long-term relationship struggles to adapt to living as a single person. Some people get into a relationship right away with the next person that they date. Other people become depressed for a couple of months or even years.

When it comes time for a transition in your life first recognize the necessity of chaos, don't fight that chaos, but instead gradually allow a new order to emerge. Figure out which aspects of your previous identity you want to preserve and which aspects of your previous identity to do away with. You can't necessarily control the new order that emerges completely, but you can guide it in the right direction. The best order to have is one which is in line with the goals of your next phase.

Chasing a Feeling

Another reason why people get stuck in a phase is due to something I call "chasing a feeling". I got this idea from the expression "chasing the dragon" which describes how heroin users go from casual use to full-blown addiction. Apparently, the first time that they use the drug they experience an incredible state of serenity which feels uniquely profound. After this experience they try heroin again, but it isn't the same. They keep using and increasing the dose in search of this first high, but they can never reach that same level. That is what is meant by "chasing the dragon".

My concept of chasing the feeling is similar. You have one experience or a series of experiences which produce a very positive and profound feeling and then as a result you try to replicate those experiences in search of that same feeling. Analogously to the first time someone uses heroin, it is impossible to replicate those rare profoundly positive experiences. It seems to me through my own life and through my conversations with other people that those sorts of profound states can't be engineered, rather they simply happen to us through some force outside of our control. Even if you find something which makes you profoundly happy in a new unique way, that profundity won't last. The act can and probably will continue to make you feel good, but not in that same profound original way.

During your experience phase you can and almost certainly will have an array of mind-blowing positive experiences which transform your conception of the world and of yourself. The tendency will be to continue to chase that original feeling. Naturally, this could keep someone in an experience phase (or any other phase) longer than they originally intended. Don't allow yourself to be controlled by a single profound experience in your life, unless it puts you on a path which is coherent with your greater aims.

***

I am seriously considering attending law school this year, which will mean sacrificing a lot of my favorite things, including traveling the world. Sure, I will still be able to travel some of the time as a lawyer, but not nearly as much. I certainly won't be able to live the same long-term travel lifestyle that I am accustomed to.

On the other hand, going into law could potentially give me a lot of opportunities and is much more in line with my current career phase. I badly want to continue traveling the world and live the nomadic lifestyle that I am used to, but I also recognize that eventually it will make more sense for me to settle down in the same place, particularly as I move into the next period of my life. The law school I am considering attending will be in one of the coldest cities in Canada so I will need to sacrifice the warm weather that I get to enjoy in tropical countries. I will also need to sacrifice my ability to move around from place to place at a moment's notice.

Fortunately, there will be a lot of positive aspects to settling down as well. Currently, since I am traveling year-round, I need to continuously rebuild my life every month or so. This means finding a new gym, a new grocery store, learning new cultural norms, finding my way around a new city etc. When I am living in the same place for a couple of years I will be able to build up a more stable routine instead of constantly creating new routines over and over again.

While I think that the minimalism I have developed during my experience phase is invaluable, I am currently only able to own those things which I can fit into my backpack, if I live in the same place I will be able to at least own a couple more items. Traveling the world I still maintain some long-term friendships, but most of my relationships with people are short-lived, longer term friendships could be another benefit of living in the same place.

There is also the factor of dealing with the potential stresses of law school and working as a lawyer. Currently, I do have to work hard, but I suspect that being a lawyer would be much more stressful. However, hard work and stress aren't the main factors that make a decision like going to law school difficult, rather it has to do with accepting a new identity. My current identity is built around pursuing interesting, exciting, or unique experiences, but the identity of a lawyer or rather the identity of someone in their career phase, is going to be much more dull and ordinary. While law in particular might not be the right choice for me, something much less exciting than my current lifestyle will likely be the best choice.

Whatever I end up doing during my career phase I will try to maintain my best habits from my experience phase. Here are some of the habits I am going to maintain in future phases, you might have some similar habits after your experience phase as well. I am listing my intentions for my next phase just to give you some ideas of what you might find useful when you are moving on from your own experience phase. Perhaps some of my intentions will be valuable for you and others won't really apply.

1. I will continue practicing the languages that I have learned and will hopefully get opportunities to learn new languages. I first learned French in Elementary school and since traveling I have developed some basic skills in a number of different languages. Currently I am in South America practicing Spanish.

2. I will keep my habit of meeting new people. As an introvert a big part of my experience phase was meeting a lot of new people. Before this period in my life I had only really interacted with people in my small friend groups and my family, since the experience phase I have met thousands of different people from all over the world in all kinds of different situations (bars, gyms, buses etc.) My intention going into my career phase is not necessarily to meet as many people as I did during my experience phase, but rather to continue to continue to meet new interesting people at least occasionally.

3. I will maintain my habit of meditating every single morning no matter what. I started meditating in 2010 and have been doing it every day since 2013. The practice keeps me grounded and serves as a daily reminder of the importance of taking on a healthy mental state. I might even meditate more often during my career phase.

4. Writing for fun is another habit I started in my experience phase which I intend on continuing into the future. I may not have as much time during my career phase for writing, but if I can squeeze in a few minutes every single day I will be satisfied.

5. I will continue to pursue new experiences. While I certainly won't be able to have as many new experiences as I did during my actual experience phase, my intention is to make sure that I am always trying new things. I don't have to do something crazy every single day, but so long as I am at least getting out of my comfort zone some of the time I know that I am doing the right thing.

While you are planning out and thinking about your next phase, I want to remind you that there is no particular phase that everyone needs to have in their life and there is no proper order to have your phases in. I am moving on to my career phase, but you might move onto a spiritual phase or a family phase after your experience phase. It depends on what you want and on what is right for you at this time in your life.

One of my biggest worries writing this book is that people will try to emulate me and have an experience phase when it isn't appropriate or feel that they should also have a career phase after their experience phase. If it is the right time in your life for a career phase be my guest, but try your best to ask yourself honestly what is truly best for you, your long-term happiness, your long-term impact, and the long-term happiness of the people around you.

This book is my best attempt to arm you with everything you need to know to start living intentionally. But, ultimately, it all comes down to you and the decisions that you make. I can try my best to imbue the things that I learnt onto you, however everyone interprets everything in their own way. Use this book as a guide, but understand that in the end it all depends on you. If there is one important thing I have learnt in my life, it is to embrace the struggle, this is the surest route to fulfillment.

Made in the USA
Lexington, KY
26 May 2019